THE REAL ESTATE AGENT'S BUSINESS PLANNER

PRACTICAL STRATEGIES FOR MAXIMIZING YOUR SUCCESS IN THE REAL ESTATE INDUSTRY

BRIDGET McCREA

This publication is designed to provide accurate and authoritative information in regard to the subject matter covered. It is sold with the understanding that the publisher is not engaged in rendering legal, accounting, or other professional services. If legal advice or other expert assistance is required, the services of a competent professional person should be sought.

Library of Congress Cataloging-in-Publication Data
McCrea, Bridget
     The real estate agent's business planner: practical strategies for maximizing your success in the real estate industry / Bridget McCrea
     p. cm.
     Includes bibliographical references
     ISBN-13: 978-0-9970454-3-7 (paperback)

© 2019 Bridget McCrea
All rights reserved
Printed in the United States of America

This publication may not be reproduced, stored in a retrieval system, reprinted or repurposed online, or transmitted in whole or in part, in any form or by any means, electronic, mechanical, photocopying, recording, or otherwise without the prior written permission of the author, Bridget McCrea.

Table of Contents

Introduction..1

CHAPTER ONE
Taking Stock..3
    The Whirlwind.................................5
    Laying It All Out...............................11
    Finding Value.................................14
    Down to Basics...............................15
    Real Estate: A Self-Driven Business..........16

CHAPTER TWO
Business Planning 101..............................21
    How Much Will You Make?..................26
    Outlining Your Key Goals...................27
    The Outline..................................28
    Key Terms Defined..........................35
    Financially Savvy............................37
    Stoking Growth..............................38

CHAPTER THREE
Developing a Marketing Plan.......................41
    Assessing the Competition..................43
    Creating Your Plan...........................46
    Real Estate Specific..........................52
    Getting Affordable...........................55
    For Existing Agents..........................58
    6 Unique Way to Find Customers for
    Your Real Estate Business...................59

CHAPTER FOUR
Treat it Like a Business 63
    It's *Not* a Job 64
    Business Sense 64
    Cash is King 68
    To Incorporate or Not? 71
    Reaping Rewards 74
    Walk the Walk 76

CHAPTER FIVE
Setting Goals and Objectives 79
    Goal Setting 101 81
    Laying it Out 82
    Food for Thought 85
    Staying Fresh 88
    Making an Entrance. 90
    Focusing Your Goals 91
    Getting Personal 93
    Setting Yourself up for Success 95
    Borrowing a Page from a Top College 96

CHAPTER SIX
Managing a Fluctuating Income 99
    The Basics 100
    Hurdling Challenges 102
    The Highs and Lows 103
    Develop a Budget 104
    Filling Your Business Pipeline. 105
    Prospect, Prospect, Prospect 108
    Cracking the Online Lead Code 109
    Tracking Your Progress 112
    Market Knowledge 112
    Get Organized 116

CHAPTER SEVEN
Tax Planning & Preparation 119
      Taxing Matters 120
      Creating a Streamlined System 122
      Estimated Tax Payments. 125
      Employer Identification Numbers 127
      1099-MISC Forms 128
      When and What to File. 128
      Hiring Help 131
      10 Tax Management Strategies for Real
      Estate Agents. 132
      Getting Going 133

CHAPTER EIGHT
Personal and Professional Development 135
      Developing Professionally 136
      Growing Your Business. 139
      Eight Team-Building Tips 141
      Going Virtual 141
      Teamwork Makes the Dream Work. 143
      Setting Priorities 144
      Time for Yourself 145
      Effective Time Management Tactics for
      Real Estate Agents 146
      Start Now 147

CHAPTER NINE
Long-Term Planning 149
      Early Steps. 152
      Strategizing for Success 154
      Other Considerations. 157
      Investing in Real Estate 159
      The Long-Term View 160
      Start Planning Today 162

APPENDIX A
Sample Business Plans 165
   Sample Business Plan #1: New Agent 165
   Sample Business Plan #2: Existing Agent 171

APPENDIX B
Business Plan Outline 179

APPENDIX C
More Business Planning Resources 181

ABOUT THE AUTHOR 183

Introduction

When my publisher first approached me about writing a business planning guide for real estate agents in 2005, the business was booming, most states were seeing run-ups in real estate values, and the industry was only just beginning to stretch its wings on the technological front. Social networking was still just a concept that someone was formulating from a college dorm, and online leads had yet to become the source of business that they are now. The industry had yet to feel the effects of the "Great Recession" and subsequent housing downturn—an experience that pushed many out of the business while opening up opportunities for a new influx of eager professionals.

A lot has changed since then, and I've been reporting on those shifts for publications like *Illinois REALTOR, Texas REALTOR, Florida REALTOR, and Real Trends.* Having interviewed dozens of agents, brokers, and real estate experts around the country over the last few years, I've learned one thing about the business: regardless of market conditions, housing starts, or generational changes, the basic tenets of real estate success are the same. Making it work is requires dedication, planning, training, sweat equity, and a good support structure.

Even in a healthy economy, the need for solid business planning to handle today's workflow and prepare adequately for the future has never been greater—both for new and existing agents. Highly cyclical in nature, the fickle real estate market could turn challenging at any moment. Through solid preparation and good strategy, you'll be more prepared for what's coming around the next corner—good, bad, or otherwise.

CHAPTER ONE
Taking Stock

Before you got into real estate, you probably had some very valid reasons for doing so. It could have been the promise of a great income, the flexible schedule that would allow you to set your own hours, the chance to work with people in your community, or the desire to learn more about the intricacies of the real estate industry. Maybe a family member was in the business, or maybe the "for sale" signs scattered around your neighborhood prompted you to look for a way to take advantage of the real estate boom.

Whatever the motivation, you most likely took a short real estate course, sat for your salesperson exam and—hopefully—became one of the roughly 45 percent of people who pass it first time out. If not, you probably took it again and passed, then hung your license at a local brokerage that met your criteria.

From that point on, your new career has probably felt a lot like a whirlwind: spending time in training classes, doing floor time, farming for clients in your neighborhood, cultivating online leads, and spending weekends showing homes. You're probably tied to your cell phone, answering each call quickly to make sure you don't miss any potential clients. You're running from one house to the next, hoping that somewhere along the way one of those contacts turns into a sale, which 30–60 days later becomes money in your pocket.

Nowhere along the way did anyone make you sit down and take a very simple entrepreneurial quiz, to make sure you're well suited for business ownership. Well, better late than never. Here's a brief one to take right now. Answer yes or no to each of the following questions:

1. Like most successful entrepreneurs, am I an optimist and a risk taker?
2. Do I have the self-starter determination to get this thing going and the discipline to keep it on track?
3. Do I work hard?
4. Can I take responsibility for my own actions?
5. Am I a good problem solver?
6. Am I organized?
7. Do I have the physical stamina to work long hours?
8. Am I willing to work weekends and evenings—the times when most homebuyers will be out looking for homes?
9. Can I finance this business myself for at least six to 12 months?
10. Will my family be supportive of my entrepreneurial efforts?
11. Do I have the basic skills required to start and successfully run a business, or do I have access to a mentor who can help me through those critical early stages?

If you answered yes to more than half of the questions, consider yourself a good candidate for a real estate career. If you answered no to five or more questions, don't despair. You may simply need to shift your approach to work, your mindset, and your way of managing tasks, challenges and problems. While no one can instill "physical stamina" and pessimists have a hard time seeing the glass as half-full, there are always experienced mentors and colleagues along with college courses to turn to for education on the fine points of running a small business. Combine those resources with a great business plan and you just may surprise yourself, your family, and your friends.

Despite the critical importance of a business plan, many entrepreneurs drag their feet when it comes to preparing a written document. They argue that their marketplace changes too fast for a business plan to be useful or that they just don't have enough time. But just as a builder won't begin construction without a blueprint, eager business owners shouldn't rush into new ventures without a business plan. Before you begin writing yours, ask yourself these four questions:

1. What service or product does your business provide and what needs does it fill?
2. Who are the potential customers for your product or service and why will they purchase it from you?
3. How will you reach your potential customers?
4. Where will you get the financial resources to start your business?

As fundamental as they may seem, these four core components are critical to your business success—whether that venture is a hair salon, a bookstore, or a new real estate practice. Know your service, your customers, how to reach them and what resources you'll need to get there, and you'll soon find yourself on the path to success.

The Whirlwind

Caught up in the whirlwind that is your new real estate career, have you stopped to do any of the following?

- Create a business plan that outlines your professional goals and aspirations, expectations, and financial needs.
- Open a business bank account in order to keep personal and business income and expenses separate.
- Set up a spreadsheet or other mechanism for tracking your work performance and resultant financial rewards.
- Develop an effective plan for marketing yourself to your potential clients.
- Map out a plan for living comfortably on a fluctuating, unpredictable income.
- After you figure out who your "ideal client" is, decide on the best approach for reaching out to that person.

- Think about how you're going to purchase your own health and life insurance.
- Decide how you'll handle long-term financial goals, such as retirement plans.
- Select a business entity—such as a sole proprietorship, corporation, S-Corp., limited liability corporation (LLC), or partnership—that best suits your business.
- Factor in issues like tax planning and preparation, since you're now an independent contractor.
- Create an action plan for personal and professional development.

If you answered no to even one of these 11 points, you'll want to take a step back and create an action plan for your business that encompasses these and other key matters. The exercise works for new and existing agents alike. For new licensees, the step probably won't have to be too big, since you're either just getting started or only a few months into it.

Existing agents may have to stretch themselves a bit further, since they've already tasted some level of success and may not see the value in a formal business planning process. For the latter, it's important to remember that it's never too late to kick off a good planning process, based on what you've already achieved and your own future aspirations in the industry.

We'll call this exercise "taking stock," and here's a worksheet that you can use to answer some key questions about yourself and your career:

1) Why did I get into the real estate business in the first place? (Were the motives financial in nature, were you looking for a new career, did you want to get out and interact with customers on a daily basis?)

_____
_____
_____
_____

2) What steps have I taken so far in my career to achieve this early goal?

3) Have I created a mission statement for my business? A good mission statement can be a foundation for assessing needs, determining objectives, setting goals, and making the daily decisions that will help you achieve success as an agent. If not, start crafting one here by answering the questions: Who am I, what am I trying to accomplish, and what do I value?

4) How do I measure success in the industry, and what specific steps do I need to take to reach that level of success in real estate?

5) How successful have I been so far in the business, and am I taking the steps outlined above to achieve my goals? Or, have I skipped steps along the way, thus lessening my chances to reach my success goals?

6) What type of marketing plan do I have in place, and does it include effective and productive marketing efforts?

_____

_____

_____

_____

7) Am I acting like a small business owner, even though I'm working for a broker? What steps have I taken so far that prove this, and what could I be doing better in this regard?

_____

_____

_____

_____

8) Where do I stand financially right now? What level of cash reserves do I have to cover my business and personal expenses for the next four to six months while I build my business?

_____

_____

_____

_____

9) In what ways do other people in my life (such as a spouse and/or children) rely on me financially? If there are no such individuals in my life, does that mean I have the luxury of spending the next few months building my business without having to worry about earning a significant level of commissions?

_____

_____

_____

_____

10) Do I have health insurance coverage for my family and myself? Do I have life insurance coverage (particularly important if you are the primary wage earner in the family)? If not, do I—as an independent contractor—have the means of getting either or both of these coverages?

_____
_____
_____

11) How will I plan the next few years of my personal and work life, factoring in issues like my children's college education, long-term care for elderly relatives, and retirement for myself?

_____
_____
_____
_____

Once you've made mental notes or jotted down answers to each of these questions, you'll also want to take some time to assess your answers and use them to help ascertain:

- Where you stand right now
- Where you want to be professionally in the next six to 12 months
- Where you want to be, both professionally and personally, in five to 10 years

Your answers to the first two "taking stock" questions will give you a good foundation to work with, even if you haven't yet laid that groundwork. Take the time to figure out the "whys" of your career choice. It could have been as simple as a friend telling you how great you would be at it, and that's fine. Then, look at the steps you've taken so far—no matter how small—to turn that idea into a reality.

For those of you who got into real estate thinking that because you hang your license at a certain brokerage you're an employee of that firm, questions #3, #6 and #7 will be particularly telling. If you haven't yet developed a mission statement for your business, and if you still feel like an employee (even though you aren't punching a clock or earning a steady paycheck), then it's time to start acting like a small business owner. It's also time to develop a marketing plan, since customers aren't (always) going to come to you. Combine time-tested strategies like farming neighborhoods for leads, asking for referrals, holding open houses, and advertising in home magazines, with newer concepts (using online lead generation services, social media, mobile marketing, QR codes, and automatic property listing alerts through your local MLS) to develop an affordable, workable plan.

Questions #4 and #5 deal with success—a fairly nebulous concept, since everyone's idea of success is different. Is success in real estate characterized by the person who has been in the industry for 20 years, closes 10 deals a month, drives a Ferrari, and vacations in St. Barts twice a year? Or is it the agent who works in the inner city, helping 10 or 12 underserved families achieve the dream of homeownership every year and volunteering his time to help build new schools in Haiti? Figure out where you fit between these two extremes, and then come up with a basic idea of how you will get there.

The last four questions are particularly important, since most agents are left to their own devices to generate business, close deals, and earn commission checks—which aren't always regular, nor are they uniform in amount. Most brokers suggest agents come into the business with four to six months' cash reserves to cover their expenses in this initial phase of operation, but those same brokers usually stress the fact that it doesn't mean it's going to take six months to start earning an income. I've heard of agents who closed deals during their first week in business, and others who took up to a year (or more) to get that first deal under their belt. A new agent's first sale is a milestone that most brokers and office managers put a lot of emphasis on, since the frustration that comes from <u>not</u> closing that first transaction can drive agents out of the business in a year or less.

The questions about health and life insurance, college savings, and retirement are equally as important, since they will get you to think past your career and assess the overall life you want to live. Since most real estate offices don't provide benefits, you'll want to check with your local and state business associations (the National Association of REALTORS® has an affiliate that offers coverage to members in certain states, for example) or try purchasing it on your own, depending on where you're located and what your specific needs are. The same goes for life insurance, and any other financial obligations that will need to be taken care of over the next five to 10 years.

Laying It All Out

Once you've taken stock of your business and personal situation, you can start planning your success in an industry where competition is stiff and the rewards that come from hard work can be handsome and varied (ranging from monetary rewards, to industry recognitions to the sheer feeling of accomplishment that comes from helping to close a difficult deal). Once you've worked your way through this book, you'll have a good handle on the following planning components:

- **Basic Business Planning:** The elements of a good plan, developing financial projections for your first (and subsequent) years in the business, reviewing and revising your plan regularly, and where to get help developing a successful business plan.

- **Your Marketing Plan:** Developing a targeted marketing plan and sticking with it, finding and cultivating a niche, budgeting for maximum effectiveness, measuring results and using that information to tweak your plan.

- **Set Goals and Objectives:** Creating attainable goals and objectives, updating those elements regularly, assessing your own needs (both personal and professional), and using that information to set goals that will help you get ahead in the field.

- **Acting Like a Business Owner:** Setting up your business structure, creating a different set of books and bank account for your company, paying yourself a paycheck (rather than just depositing commission checks into your personal account), and the value of creating banking relationships and joining trade organizations.

- **Manage a Fluctuating Income:** Taking steps that will help even out the fluctuations, dealing with them in an effective manner when the checks do ebb and flow, and creating budgets that ensure your long-term financial success in the industry.

- **Tax Planning:** Budgeting for taxes, making estimated tax payments, finding a good accountant to handle your tax preparation and year-round planning, working with a financial planner on longer-term tax planning issues.

- **Personal and Professional Development:** Learning to prioritize, enriching yourself through continuing education and certifications, supporting and growing your business, creating an overall sales strategy for your business, knowing when to hire help, join forces with a partner, or form a team and running a business that is not only financial rewarding, but also enjoyable and fulfilling.

- **Planning for the Long-Term:** Developing a "big picture" view of your career and finances, taking care of important issues like health and life insurance, saving for retirement and college savings, and planning not only for your next big sale, but also for the next 5–10 years of your life.

At this point, you may be asking yourself: Isn't this an awful lot of planning? Yes, it is, but the good news is that this book will help you break down the process into manageable chunks. It's designed to hit the areas of highest to least priority for the typical agent, although not everyone will approach the planning process in the same fashion. For example, a single mother who just got licensed could be more concerned about managing a fluctuating income, while a married agent who is just starting a family might be more concerned about being able to establish a college fund for his first child.

To get the most out of your planning, you'll want to follow these basic guidelines:

- **Start at Square One:** Begin with some business planning basics, and outline your overall plan first before going back and beefing up areas of most concern for your particular situation.

- **Do Your Homework:** Put some time into researching your market, your potential customers, and your own financial situation to come up with a realistic picture of where you are right now, where you want to be, and how you're going to get there.

- **Write It Down:** Don't try to commit everything to memory. Jot down notes as you think through your situation and your future goals and dreams, then use those notes to create a written business plan.

- **Network, But Do Your Own Thing:** You can learn a lot from existing agents, but no single agent's plan is going to be right for another. As you pick the brains of those around you for ideas, select those that sound most and discard the rest. Then, use the best of the best to develop your own plan.

- **Update Regularly:** Like life, a business plan is a work in progress. You'll want to review your overall plan at least yearly, if not on a quarterly basis, to make sure you're on track. If you've met your goals, revise them. If you're much further off than you thought you would be, you may want to make the goals more attainable and tangible.

- **Make the Time For It:** The beauty of small business planning is that it costs little more than time. And while it's true that new agents are usually time strapped—trying to start their careers, find customers, and make money—it will pay to go through this early planning exercise before you get too far into it. The same goes for the existing agent who has never taken the time to plan.

Finding Value

In many cases, the planning process itself can be more valuable than the paper or digital plan that comes out of it. Preparing a sound business plan requires time and effort, but the benefits greatly exceed the costs. Building the plan forces a potential entrepreneur to look at her business idea in the harsh light of reality, and requires the owner to assess the company's chances of success more objectively.

"The real value in preparing a business plan is not so much in the plan itself as it is in the process the entrepreneur goes through to create the plan," says one professor of entrepreneurship at a large U.S. college. "Although the finished product is useful, the process of building a plan requires an entrepreneur to subject his idea to an objective, critical evaluation. What he learns about his company, its target market, its financial requirements, and other factors can be essential to his success."

Unfortunately, most businesspeople don't recognize the value of working through the planning process. Real estate agents are notorious for breezing through their educational courses, zipping through their exam, loading up on business cards, and hitting the street to try to make some money. Some have certainly succeeded with this gung-ho attitude, but many more find themselves bogged down by the complexities of doing business in a challenging career where the barriers to entry are fairly low and the obstacles to success can be difficult to overcome. Instead of stopping to take a breath, they plod along, hoping for success.

Others do take the time to plan, but they use ineffective strategies for doing so. For example, downloading a business planning program and answering all of the questions that it throws at you doesn't guarantee that you'll end up with a good plan. While such programs can help you get your ducks lined up and your brain in "planning" mode, it takes more than just a computer program to create a plan for real estate success.

Down to Basics

You don't need a course to get started on your own business plan. Just be sure you include the following:

- **Budget:** Start with a basic personal budget so you know what you need to survive during your first one to two years in business. Then, develop a separate business budget that factors in your own finances, since the two will probably be intertwined during your "startup" phase. Most importantly, be honest and realistic and gain a clear understanding of your own monthly financial needs for your first year.

- **Goal Setting:** This is a key step for new agents, who must know what their goals are if they expect to be able to meet them. A few concrete goals that you can set as an agent are:

    I plan to have my interviews completed by _____.

    I plan to have my license placed by _____.

    Therefore, I should have my first commission check by _____.

    Which means I should have my first sale by _____.

- **A Support Team:** This team should be made up of your broker (for marketing tools, office space, support, and training), a mortgage lender (who can pre-qualify your prospects, take buyers' applications, and order appraisals) and a title company (to conduct title searches, order termite inspections, and prepare closing documents). Your support team is vital to your success. It will help you in more ways than you can imagine when prospects are hard to qualify for a mortgage or the closing starts falling apart. Once your career advances and you can afford to expand, you'll probably want to add a sales assistant, a transaction coordinator, and other support personnel to your team.

- **Learn the Real Estate Lingo:** The sooner you learn how to "talk the talk" in real estate, the better off you will be. Here are a few to help you get started:

  Addendum: Any additional documents that go into a real estate contract.

  Appraisal: How a loan officer determines if the property is worth as much (or as little) as the buyer has offered on it.

  Closing: When the buyer's purchase will be recorded by the county and become their property.

  CMA: A report that shows prices of homes that are comparable to a subject home and that were recently sold, are for sale now, or that were taken off the market.

  Contingency: Something that has to fulfilled in order for another event to take place.

  Escrow: A financial instrument held by a third party for the two other parties (usually buyer and seller) in a transaction.

  Pre-Qualified: When a buyer submits a loan application to a lender before the home-buying process starts (versus a pre-approval, which shows that the buyer has actually secured the funding).

Real Estate: A Self-Driven Business

For any plan to be effective, it must incorporate not only your work life, but also your family life and your personal goals and dreams. Notorious for working around the clock, seven days a week, real estate agents are particularly prone to getting caught up in the "all work and no play" way of life. Avoiding this vicious cycle can be as simple as scheduling your kid's soccer games in your calendar, just as you would an appointment, or hiring a part-time assistant to manage client communications and field their requests.

As you embark on your real estate career (or, as you grow your existing business) such suggestions may seem trivial, but they are important. Most real estate agents are "doers." They're quick to volunteer, get involved with their communities and even run for public office. They help out at their children's schools, assist homebuyers during the moving process, and do errands for clients when needed. Too often, they turn into "over-doers" because they've never taken the time to plan. As a result, they miss a few critical areas of the business startup process, like:

- Collecting critical market information that will lead to competitive advantages, lucrative niches, and the ability to tap market trends that their competitors may be unaware of.
- Focusing their activities to maximize the available tools, programs, resources, advice, and materials.
- Understanding the industry as a whole and how it operates, which in turn enhances their ability to anticipate and deal with business challenges as they crop up.
- Gaining introspection about goals and aspirations, both personal and professional.

Of course, many agents cruise along in the industry without doing much planning. Usually these folks have a large network of friends, family, and colleagues to keep their pipelines full. They may also have family members who have been in the business, shown them the ropes, and pointed business in their direction. The rest of the agents who are competing for business in the real world, however, would achieve much faster and efficiently if they had a plan of action in place before getting in too deep.

The good news is that planning doesn't have to be expensive or time consuming. The better news is that any amount of time or money that you put into it is sure to pay off tenfold. In fact, most sales associates in the real estate industry fail due to a lack of written objectives, a lack of structure and self-discipline in their daily activities, and a lack of ongoing training and support.

"Real estate is a self-driven business," says one management consultant who has been working with agents for over 30 years. "An agent must develop a KISS (keep it simple stupid) business plan and relentlessly stick to it."

For agents, keeping it simple means committing a few key tenets to memory. Here are a few to start with, though you may have a few of your own to add to the list:

- Treat your real estate career as a business.
- Create a successful business plan and a budget, then live by them.
- Tweak those plans as needed, to adjust to changes in your business or life.
- Realize that you have to spend money to make money, and don't be afraid to buy a tech tool or device that will help you more productively generate new or manage existing business.
- Pinpoint a salary level that you need to achieve, then work backwards to figure out how many sales you need to meet that income requirement.
- Separate work and play. It's not always easy to do in real estate with a cell phone attached to your hip, but take an intentional day or two off every week—just like you would in a 9–5 job.
- Be realistic about your real estate career. Understand that it could be a few years before you can afford the luxury foreign car or the waterfront home that the more experienced agent at the office is bragging about.
- Don't be discouraged by small setbacks, and instead chalk them up to experience and use that knowledge to navigate future business dealings.

With this book as your guide, you'll be able to do all of this and more. You'll learn all about business planning fundamentals and review a sample plan to determine the best format for your own plan.

> **Don't Make These Three Mistakes!**
>
> In a YouTube video, CA Realty Training Head Trainer and Owner Robert Rico recounts the biggest mistakes made in his real estate career, and what he learned from them. Here are three things he tells new agents to avoid:
>
> **Lack of follow-up.** Ensuring every part of the transaction is processed and approved is vital to closing every deal you make. That's why following up will help you guarantee that everything is done right. You can't afford to leave any mistakes behind. Accidentally emailing the wrong person or forgetting to process a documentation are unprofessional errors that can be fixed by double–or triple–checking your work. When you take time to do something, make sure you take time to do it right the first time.
>
> **Poor financial planning.** Keeping a tab on your finances prevents you from burning through your funds. Practicing good financial habits will help you survive your real estate career. That's why creating budgets, researching how to cut costs, and putting money away for a rainy day will help you save. When you're saving money, you won't burn out in your career.
>
> **Bad time management.** Time management is an underrated trait. New real estate agents will find the flexible and lucrative lifestyle auspicious. They'll take advantage of not having a strict schedule enforced by a boss. When you schedule, prioritize work, and set deadlines for yourself, you'll turn into a proactive, productive machine. All it takes is a little initiative to build up the right momentum.
>
> *See the full list of recommendations and watch Robert's video at: https://www.carealtytraining.com/new-real-estate-agents-mistakes/*

Once you've read through this book and worked through some of the accompanying checklists, quizzes, and bonus materials, your personal and professional picture will be much more focused. You'll also have at your fingertips the basic information necessary to create a business plan that will help you shape the future of your business. Are you ready to get started? Great, now just turn the page.

CHAPTER TWO

Business Planning 101

Most new agents are afraid of the amount of time it takes to create a written business plan, but those who do spend the time—and the experts who advocate this step—agree that the payoff is well worth it. In fact, a business plan helps agents focus in an environment where it's very easy to get pulled off in many different directions. Having a solid plan in place helps both new and experienced agents focus on what they need to be doing on a daily basis in order to earn their incomes.

Of the many new and experienced agents that one Texas broker hires annually, she estimates that *75 percent lack a solid business plan.* Ignoring this step trips up all agents, but can be particularly harmful to the new agent that doesn't factor in licensing fees and MLS dues, and winds up in the hole financially before her first commission check is cut.

The good news is that getting started with a business plan is simple enough. All it takes is a first draft (go ahead and scribble it on a cocktail napkin!) to break through the writer's block. When it's time to take this step, look first at these four important areas:

1. A description of your business and business activities
2. A brief outline of your marketing plan (see Chapter Three for more in-depth discussion on creating a marketing plan)
3. The financing details: How will you finance your business, and what will that initial investment cover?

4. The management aspect: How will you manage your business through the first six to 12 months of its life?

It's important to consider all four of these steps because they will blend together to help you manage your successful real estate career. Without a good idea of exactly what you're doing and what marketing strategies you'll use to achieve your goals, for example, you'll never really know if you're reaching those aspirations (or not). And, if you don't address your own financial capabilities and obstacles early in the game, shepherding your business through that first year is going to be a struggle.

Depending on the information source, 85–90 percent of new real estate agents leave the business within their first five years. That's because even in a world where facilitating 6- and 7-figure transactions logically translates into a lucrative career choice, it still takes years to build a successful business and earn a good living.

According to the National Association of REALTORS®' most recent numbers, the median gross income of REALTORS was $39,800 in 2017, down from $42,500 in 2016. (Note that this measure is the amount that divides the income distribution into two equal groups—half of agents have an income <u>above</u> that amount and the other half have an income that falls <u>below</u> that amount). NAR doesn't publish average salary numbers, but according to PayScale, the average pay for a REALTOR is $54,175 per year.

NAR says that the income levels of "new members entering the field" depend on experience, function, and hours worked per week. Sixty percent of members who have two years or less experience made less than $10,000 in 2017, for example, compared to 40 percent of members with more than 16 years of experience (who made more than $100,000 in the same time period). Agents with 16 years or more experience had a median gross income of $78,850—up from $73,400 in 2015, NAR reports.

To make these numbers, REALTORS close a median number of 11 transaction sides annually. Most worked 40 hours per week in 2017, a trend that has continued for several years, according to NAR. The typical agent earned 12 percent of his or her business from repeat clients and customers, with 17 percent through referrals from past clients and customers.

With these numbers in mind, we're going to concentrate on the dollars and cents of the real estate business, although we will help you create a complete business plan later in the chapter. You don't want to find yourself staring at an empty bank balance when you're just 30 days away from your first commission check, so take the early steps necessary to make sure that doesn't happen.

To make sure he didn't wind up being one of the majority of agents who throw in the towel before getting a taste of success, one agent took an honest look at his own financial picture and decided how to finance both his new real estate career and lifestyle during the startup phase of his new business.

In need of help, he signed up for a local firm's "basic training" course. From it, he took away a range of valuable strategies and tools to use in the field. He considers one of the most important to be the "Survival Business Plan" spreadsheet, on which he was able to map out his entire financial year prior to picking up the phone to call his first client.

"It was a real eye opener for me," says the agent. "It showed me how to plan for success in this business." He started by filling in an entire year's worth of data on his personal or "family" finances and liabilities (mortgage payments, food expenses, etc.) as well as business expenses (association dues, training costs, technology expenses, etc.). The exercise showed him in exactly what timeframe he needed to make his first sale, how long his personal or family reserves would last, how much positive cash flow he would have by the end of his first year in the business, plus other valuable insights.

Because this agent analyzed his own finances and capabilities <u>before</u> going into real estate on a full-time basis, he gained a clear view of exactly what needs to be done not only to survive, but also to thrive in the competitive real estate business. During his first six months in the business he closed three transactions and was already working on five active listings. He broke even during that first year, and was on track for a 20 to 25 percent gain in profits during his second year in the business.

"I used a very realistic, spreadsheet-based plan that showed me exactly where I was at financially, where I needed to be in six months, and what I needed to do to get there," says the agent. "I know that I need to list a certain number of homes and complete a specific number of sales per month to reach my goals, and that's exactly what I'm doing."

The Survival Business Plan was developed by a 30-year real estate veteran and coach who helps agents drill in one crucial starting point: Know and understand your finances before you get into the real estate business. That means knowing:

- How much cash you have in reserve
- How much money your spouse or significant other is making each month
- How much commission you can reasonably expect during your first six to 12 months in business

Those income numbers are then offset by expenses that include car insurance, car payments, mortgage payments, and homeowner's insurance on the family side; and marketing expenses, technology costs, and other overhead needed to run your business. From there, new agents can estimate their monthly cash flow and determine how many closings, sales, and prospects they need to get each month to reach a positive cash flow.

"New agents really need to understand the financial implications of their undertaking, but most don't," the coach says. Because most new agents work solely on commissions, they must have at least some level of cash reserve saved <u>before</u> getting started. Realize that the industry's median gross income is $39,800 and factor that into your projections to figure out whether you can afford to put all of your time into real estate.

To increase on these average salary projections, agents need to figure out their prospect-to-sales ratio and improve on it over time.

To make that happen, real estate agents must get a handle on the following key aspects of their careers:

- Know their finances
- Learn how to sell
- Stay focused on their careers
- Not lose their vision for success
- Do their homework
- Interview at least three real estate offices before choosing a broker
- Read the broker's policy manual
- Thoroughly understand the compensation setup (which varies from office to office)
- Stick with your decision in a positive, focused manner
- Dig deep into their circles of influence to jumpstart their careers and get those early "wins" on the board
- Explore new lead-generation activities (social networking, online leads, etc.)

Now, you probably are already getting the message loud and clear that agents will greatly increase their chances of succeeding in real estate by getting an early handle on their finances and by using that information to make first-year projections. The problem is that too many agents are working under extreme financial pressure, which multiplies every other problem by at least 10 times, the coach points out. "But if agents possess the financial strength and a good solid plan there's no reason they shouldn't be extremely successful in the business within a two- to three-year period, depending on how hard and smart they work."

And while a business plan covers different aspects of running a business, the financial planning that an agent will have to go through during the process will by far be the most valuable part of the plan. Agents need to know how much reserve they need for the first six months to one year, plain and simple. The problem is that many new agents overlook expenses like REALTOR association dues and advertising costs when considering their startup fees. A few hundred dollars per month for such expenses may sound doable when you're sitting in real estate school, but these charges can add up quickly and negatively impact the bank account of a new agent who is still working toward her first commission check.

Once a plan is in place, agents can also more effectively manage cash flow (instead of spending an entire commission check within a day of receiving it) because they're innately aware of what expenses they need to cover, how much to keep for themselves and how much to allocate for taxes. Without these solid numbers in mind, an agent's dreams and aspirations can quickly dissolve into stressful, frustrating situations—particularly if that agent's significant other suffers a job loss, his home needs a new roof, or he wants to take a family vacation.

"There are real-life pressures associated with any commission-only job, and they have to be dealt with early on, as opposed to later," says the coach. "Once an agent is out in the field, under pressure to perform, it will be hard to deal with issues like debt and financial woes. Sometimes the only option is to get out of the business and go back to a full-time, salaried, or hourly position."

How Much Will You Make?

Before you start putting any financial projections down on paper, you'll want to have a solid grasp on just how your commissions break down. Realize that a 3 percent commission (for handling either the buy or sell side of the transaction) on a $150,000 home doesn't necessarily equate to a $4,500 commission check. You must also factor the broker's cut, expenses, and dues into the equation. Here's how it all breaks down on the typical $200,000 sale:

>   a) Home sales price: $200,000 (we'll just use the average home sales price in the U.S. as a baseline)
>
>   b) Sales Commission of 3 percent: $6,000 (based on a total 6 percent commission)

c) Less Franchise Fee of 6 percent: $360 (plug your specific franchise fee in here)

d) Proceeds after franchise fee: $5,640

e) Your split: (based on a 50/50 arrangement) $2,820 (factor in your specific arrangement here)

f) Marketing Fee: $100 a month (marketing and desk fees are usually paid monthly, whether you make a sale or not)

g) Proceeds after marketing fee: $2,720

h) E & O Insurance: $40 per sale (usually paid per sale)

i) Your check amount: $2,680

j) Less prepaid training fees and other charges (we'll approximate $300 here)

l) Your total paycheck: $2,380 (and sorry, but don't forget Uncle Sam's portion)

As you can see, it's important to keep the momentum going in real estate. Unless you're planning to be a part-time agent, closing one deal and then taking a vacation until the next one comes along isn't going to be an option. For at least the first few years in business, you're going to have to put as much time, effort, and sweat equity into your career in order to make it financially viable.

Outlining Your Key Goals

The good thing about goals is that they're completely measurable. You may have no idea how many prospects you need before you make a sale, but you'll get better with time. A good rule of thumb is to assume that you'll need 10 prospects for every closed sale.

Agents should fill in the following worksheet during the planning process, then refer to it regularly to make sure they're meeting or beating their initial projections:

1. I plan to have my broker interviews completed by _____

2. I plan to have my license placed by _____

3. Therefore, I should have my first commission check by _____

4. Which means I should have my first sale by _____

5. Since my first commission check will average about _____ and will close 30 days from the contract date I need to make my first sale by _____(Month)

6. This means I must talk to_____ qualified prospects by _____

The Outline

Business plans range in size and scope from a few sheets of paper to the book you're reading right now. It all depends on how much time and effort you want to put into it, and what you want to get out of it. Somewhere in between is probably best, with the words and figures organized in a logical, understandable fashion.

For help, you might want to check out one of the many online business planning programs, apps and samples. Not all of them will be relevant to the real estate business and some may not be thought-provoking enough to create a viable plan, since your status as a real estate agent is very different from any other kind of business. On one hand, you're accountable to a higher power (namely your broker, followed by your state's real estate associations and licensing entities), yet on the other you will be operating in a largely independent manner. Put simply, you make or break yourself. This is both an opportunity and a challenge, and it can be particularly daunting for someone who has never run their own business before.

Even the sample real estate business plans published on the U.S. Small Business Administration's website are geared more toward opening a brokerage, rather than starting up as a sales associate. With that in mind, we'll take a look at a basic business plan (which you can adapt to your specific business), along with any relevant, industry-specific notes and advice where applicable.

Before you sit down to write out your hopes, dreams, and plans, it may help to envision an audience for your masterpiece—someone else reading your plan (such as an investor, or a bank that you've approached for a line of credit)—while you're writing it. This will help ensure that the document is both clear and concise, and that no important elements are overlooked. If you need help filling in any of the sections, check the appendix of this book for a sample new agent, existing agent, and brokerage business plan:

1. **Cover Sheet:** This page should reflect the image of your new company, and include any logos or graphics that you plan to use during the course of business. Use "Business Plan for _____ Company" as the title, and be sure to date the plan.

2. **Table of Contents:** For future reference and for the sake of others who will read your plan, be sure to list each section and sub-section throughout the plan.

3. **Executive Summary:** This is a one- to two-page summary of your business plan, so you may want to write it after you've completed the rest of the document. Summarize the key points covered in the plan, and include a complete-but-brief overview of your plan. You'll also want to discuss your new business and your goals, such as: "I will hang my license at ABC Realty, Inc., and become an independent contractor working under the broker of record at this agency, serving as a trusted advisor and facilitator for buyers and sellers of residential real estate. My goal is to work as either a buyer's agent (working solely with buyers), seller's agent (working solely with those consumers wishing to list their homes) or a combination of the two, and to close X number of transaction sides (the buy or sell side of the deal) annually in order to earn X number of dollars in commissions a year."

4. **Industry/Market Analysis:** When you write this section, pretend that the person who reads your plan knows nothing

about your firm or its industry. Make it as basic as possible, and answer the following questions:

   a. What is the size of the industry? (Measured by data like the number of existing and new homes sold in your area in a given year, population growth, etc.)

   b. How quickly is the industry growing? (You can usually obtain such statistics from your local Multiple Listing Service [MLS] or REALTOR organization)

   c. What are the typical profit margins? (Or, how much can you expect to pocket on any given deal after paying your broker's cut and any expenses?)

   d. Who are the major players in the industry?

   e. What are some of the trends and forecasts for the industry? (NAR and most state and local REALTOR associations track key data pertaining to the real estate field.)

   f. What changes are occurring in the industry that will create new opportunities for companies such as yours? (The proliferation of discount and Internet brokers, for example, has spawned a new interest in experience, full-service brokers.)

5. **Business Overview:** Describe the products or services that you'll be selling (which in your case will mainly be helping people buy and sell homes), how long your firm has been operating, and a few of its short-term and long-term business goals. Focus on brief, concise descriptions in this section, and keep it limited to one or two pages. Avoid a lot of industry jargon, and—as suggested earlier—write it for someone who knows nothing about real estate. If you're going to use your business plan to seek out financing or backing, you'll also want to detail what the funds will be used for (office equipment, vehicle, website development, first year's worth of rent, etc.).

6. **Ownership and Legal Structure:** This will be the easy part for most agents since it's pretty customary to start out as a sole proprietor. However, as you grow your career you'll probably reach a point where incorporating or starting a partnership may make sense. When this happens, you'll adjust your plan to reflect this new status. In Chapter Four (Treat It Like a Business) you'll find more in-depth discussion on incorporating and business structures.

7. **Management and Staffing:** The good news is that if you stick with and grow your real estate business, all of the duties outlined here won't fall on your shoulders forever. Real estate "teams" (in which a number of licensed and non-licensed professionals band together and share the duties) are a popular choice for agents who are in "growth mode," as is the hiring of full- and part-time assistants and even virtual assistants. Start this section with a short paragraph detailing your own staffing aspirations (even if you're a one-man-show right now), describe what roles those team members or employees will fill in your growing business and detail your plans for adding human resources to your operation as it grows and prospers.

8. **Marketing Plan:** This section is particularly important for real estate agents, who can't just sit around their offices, waiting for customers to walk in the door. Competition is too stiff and there are entirely too many real estate offices vying for buyers' and sellers' business to operate in this fashion. Chapter Three of this book is devoted to your marketing plan, but for now it's important to start thinking about these details:

    a. What you're selling

    b. Why customers want and/or need it

    c. What value you bring to the table (why should buyers and sellers pick you over any other agent?)

    d. How you will reach those customers

e. How you will do business with those customers
   f. How your services will be priced
   g. What your competition looks like
   h. Your competitive advantage

9. **Operational Plan:** This section is geared more towards product businesses (such as manufacturers), but is still applicable to real estate agents, who <u>should factor in these points</u>:
   a. Who will run the business?
   b. Where will the company will be based?
   c. Where will the work be done? (at the office, at home, at Starbucks, etc.)
   d. The tools, resources, and technology you'll use to work as efficiently as possible.
   e. What tools or resources you'll need, and which ones you already have, to run the business.

10. **Financial Plan:** Kick this section off with the words "level of funding needed" to get the business rolling or growing, and go from there. Fill in an honest assessment of how much money you'll need to get this business off the ground and exactly how you'll use that money. If you have any historical financial statements (i.e., the past three years' balance sheets and income statements), include them. You'll also want to develop two to three years' worth of projections, based on the goals and action steps that you wrote down and reviewed earlier in this chapter.

11. **Business strengths and weaknesses:** Do an honest assessment of yourself. What's great and innovative about what you're doing, what makes you stand out in the marketplace, and where can you use some help? Stick to three or four solid strengths that will make you stand out in the marketplace, and be as specific as possible. Rather than writing down a statement like, "I pro-

vide great customer service" write, "I will lease a moving van at moment's notice and loan it to a customer for use during the moving process." Be equally as specific about your weaknesses, and then think about what you can do to overcome these issues. If you're time-strapped and unable to answer email within a few hours, for example, your solution may be to hire a part-time assistant to handle your non-core tasks.

12. **Growth projections:** Start by answering these questions:
    - Where do I see my company and myself in one year?
    - Where will I be in five years?
    - How will I get there?
    - Are these goals attainable in my industry? (Do some research, talk to other agents and brokers, and form a consensus based on input from a number of different sources.)
    - Can my market support these growth projections? (Research your market by looking at new home building, sales growth of existing homes, and number of new agents/brokers that come into the business on an annual basis)
    - Will I need to cultivate new niches (such as working with single, millennial, senior, or international homebuyers) to reach my goals?
    - What type of year-over-year sales increases and growth projections will come as a result of my taking these steps?

13. **Exit Strategy:** Any business expert will tell you that having a Plan B and even a Plan C can mean the difference between success and failure in the business world. Creating an exit strategy early in the process doesn't mean you're ready to give up. It means you're ready to embrace anything that comes your way, and that you're truly ready to treat your practice like a business, and not a hobby.

"An exit strategy is critical, but it's something that very few entrepreneurs think about when they're writing their first business plan," says one professor of entrepreneurship at a large U.S. college. "They're so concerned with getting their companies off the ground, and making payroll, that they overlook the need for an exit strategy."

Here are a few quick tips for creating an exit strategy:

- If you can't lay out an exit strategy in writing, at least have a few alternative plans in mind, should things not go as intended with your new business.
- Consult with an attorney, CPA, financial planner, or other professional (preferably a team of professionals) to help develop a viable exit strategy.
- Take the time to develop an exit strategy, even if you have to take a few hours or days away from your day-to-day business operations to do it. It will pay off.
- Don't forget to sit down and talk with your spouse and/or family members (particularly those who work or have a stake in the business) before creating your exit strategy.
- Create an exit strategy as early as possible (preferably when you draw up your first business plan) then tweak it as necessary as your company blossoms and grows.

Along with the items in the detailed business plan you just read through, you may want to also incorporate one or more of the following points in your business plan:

- Protection such as licenses, trademarks, or copyrights
- Timing of major operations, such as a business expansion, hiring of employees, forming a team, or launching your website
- A set of assumptions, such as anticipated sales volume, cost of goods sold and gross profit, and data from trade associations

(home sales, new home sales, number of competitors in the market)

- Projected income statements, monthly for three to five years, then quarterly for three to five years

- Projected cash flow statements monthly for two years, and quarterly for the following three to five years

- A break-even analysis for your business, showing at exactly what point you will reach profitability. For some agents, this can come as quickly as two months into the business. For others, it may take six to 12 months to reach this level.

Key Terms Defined

Here are the definitions of a few key financial terms that you'll want to be familiar with:

Cash Flow Statement: This is a projection of your business's cash inflows and outflows over a certain period of time. A typical cash flow statement predicts the anticipated cash receipts and disbursements of a business on a month-to-month basis, but can also be created on a weekly or daily basis. Because cash flow in the real estate industry is usually uncertain—particularly during the startup phase—you won't want to look so far into the future that predictions become inaccurate.

Income Statement: Also known as a Profit and Loss statement (P&L), this document lists your business' income, expenses, and net income (or loss). The net income (or loss) is equal to your income minus your expenses.

Balance Sheet: This is a financial snapshot of your business at a given date in time. The balance sheet includes your assets and liabilities, and your company's net worth. It generally includes the following information, which is then calculated to come up with a "total liabilities and capital," number:

Assets

Current Assets

Cash on hand
Accounts Receivable (less reserve for bad debts)
Merchandise Inventory (generally not applicable for a real estate business)
Prepaid Expenses
Notes Receivable

Fixed Assets

Vehicles (less accumulated depreciation)
Furniture and Fixtures (less accumulated depreciation)
Equipment (less accumulated depreciation)
Buildings and Land (generally not applicable for a real estate agent)

Other Assets

Liabilities and Capital

Current Liabilities:

Accounts Payable
Sales Taxes Payable
Payroll Taxes Payable
Accrued Wages Payable
Unearned Revenues
Short-Term Notes Payable
Short-Term Bank Loan Payable

Long-Term Liabilities:

Long-Term Notes Payable
Mortgage Payable

Capital:

Owner's Equity
Net Profit

Once you've completed your business plan, you'll want to review it with a friend, business associate, colleague, CPA, or other trusted advisor. The business plan is a flexible document that should change as your business grows. It can be used to get financing, take your firm to the next level, or to simply help you feel confident in your own ability to run a business. Treat it like a first draft, and use the feedback gathered to create a final document.

Financially Savvy

I can't stress enough how important it is to know and understand your finances before you get into the real estate business. I can name at least three friends who, just in the last few years, got into real estate and learned quickly that it takes time for those commission checks to start flowing. In the meantime, all three struggled under varying degrees of financial pressure. You can avoid this by:

- Knowing how much cash you have in reserve right now.
- Figuring out how much money your spouse or significant other is earning each month.
- Taking a realistic look at how much commission you can reasonably expect to make during your first six to 12 months in business.

Remember that these and other financial expenses will offset your projected income numbers:

- Mortgage payments
- Car payments
- Auto, home and other insurance bills
- Marketing expenses for your business
- Phone bills
- Technology tools, applications, and software
- MLS and association fees
- Office rent (if you've signed with a 100 percent commission firm, for example)

With these financials in mind, you'll be able to create a monthly cash flow and determine how many closings, sales, and prospects you need every month to reach a positive cash flow. By using tools like Excel spreadsheets that outline the financial factors mentioned above, agents can gain a foothold in the industry whether they have past sales experience or not. Do your homework, interview at least three offices before making your choice, then read the broker's policy manual thoroughly before hanging your license on the wall. Then stick with your decision in a positive, focused manner.

Stoking Growth

Existing agents need good business planning too. And while they may not necessarily have to go through the basic hoops that new agents would, these seasoned veterans should take quarterly and annual snapshots of their progress and come up with ways to keep their careers growing in the right direction.

For example, look first at the number of closed transactions for the prior year by property address. You want to know if the commission was generated from the buyer side or listing side, what the sales price was, and the amount of commission earned. From this you can determine your average sales price.

Next, examine just the number listings taken for the prior year. Again, you want to note these by property address, date sold, or time taken off the market and the reason that a property didn't sell. This will tell you the percentage of listings sold compared to listings taken, and will help you determine exactly how productive you've been over the last few months.

Lastly, look at your sources of business. Determine this by listings taken and also by buyer-controlled sales. Note by property address what the source of the business was (a farm, FSBO, referral, etc.), and after you've gathered the data, use this worksheet to analyze it:

Business Analysis Year _____
Total Commission Earned (gross)_____

Listing Side:
Number of Listings Taken_____
Number of Listings Sold_____
Percentage of Listing Sold to Listings Taken (line 3 divided by line 2) _____

Total Volume of Listings Sold_____
Average Sales Price_____

Selling Side:
Number of Buyer-Controlled Sales_____
Total Volume of Buyer-Controlled Sales_____
Average Sales Price of Buyer-Controlled Sales_____

Unit Totals:
Number of Listings Sold_____
Number of Buyer-Controlled Sales_____
Total Closed Units_____

Average Income Per Unit:
Total Commissions Earned_____
Total Closed Units_____
Average Commission Earned Per Unit_____
Percentage of Business from Listings Sold_____
Percentage of Business from Buyer Controlled Sales_____

Now that you know where you have been, you can start planning. Did most of your sales come from your sold listings? Did you get your listings from farming? Or, were you equal in listings and buyer-controlled sales? Were there many referrals? Where did they come from?

"It's so much easier to plan if you can see an analysis of past performance right in front of you," says one management consultant. "You'll also want to look at your expenses. Do they correlate with where your business comes from? In other words, are you spending the most in an area where you are getting the most business?" If not, consider spending more in areas where you get your business and less in other areas. In return, you should see your firm's revenue go up and expenses level off.

Don't forget to look at your marketplace, and any changes that may have taken place within that market over the last 12 months. Is it similar to last year? Do you think that doing the same activities will net you the same result? If you do not add to your activities, you can bet that you will not increase your revenue. The key is to put your marketing dollars where you get the most business. Increase your activities there, but don't try to spend more in other areas when you are *obviously getting good results from a specific area.*

Now, good planning is more than just getting words on paper or on your mobile device. It requires thought and should prompt you to think about your business and its future. Use a calendar to plan your activities, your spending, and your time, and remember that you only have 24 hours in a day to do all of these business activities <u>and</u> live your life.

"Creating your own business plan doesn't have to take weeks or months, but it does have to incorporate some analysis of what you are doing," says the management consultant. "The best performers plan. I coach top agents to spend one to three days on the process, brainstorming and getting focused on what will bring them the most rewards—including both sales and time off."

Those brainstorming sessions usually surprise agents, as most had an idea of where their business was coming from, but never took the time to sit down and really figure out their sources of income and whether their marketing and advertising investments were actually paying off, and contributing to those income streams. "When you have a business plan written down, along with your goals for the next 12 months," the consultant advises, "you have all the makings for a tremendously successful year."

CHAPTER THREE

Developing a Marketing Plan

Every good real estate agent has a marketing plan in place. It could be a well-defined, documented plan or a mental awareness as to which three marketing tools work best for that agent and why. Because your marketing plan communicates how you will reach your customer, you'll want to put some extra emphasis into this section of your business plan. In this chapter, we break the "marketing" section of your business plan into a separate entity, since it's such an integral part of any agent's success.

Of course, having an overall business plan is one thing, but in real estate a marketing plan can play a critical role in an agent's success. It's easy to get caught up in all of the new options, gadgets and gizmos available on the market today without properly assessing each of them. As a result, agents end up throwing money and valuable time out the window in their quest to find the best marketing tactic, most effective advertising method or best promotional tool.

When creating your plan—something most agents will tell you that they've done, even if they haven't—remember that it's not really a plan unless it's written down. You need a well-thought out, strategic business plan committed in writing, before you can do anything else. Consider any other small business. Say you were opening a store or a restaurant and seeking a bank loan to help get it off the ground. The first thing the bank is going to ask for is to see your business plan, *yet very few real estate agents have a written plan in place.*

Planning is crucial in many ways, and helps agents hone the following key points before getting into business:

- It helps you set goals for yourself.
- It provides specific direction for your business.
- It helps you get a handle on exactly where your business is headed.
- It provides a roadmap for where you're going and how you're going to get there.

"Without a plan," says one long-time real estate coach, "agents often end up jumping from one strategy to another and never making any real progress as a result." And while a complete business plan is important, the marketing component is particularly crucial for agents. It's equally as important for large companies. "Marketing is at the root of the success for many of today's leading companies," he notes.

For agents, marketing is about creating an image and consistently delivering that message to a desired audience. When homeowners continue to receive your materials, you're planting that seed in their heads. "Maybe they're not going to move for five years. Maybe they're going to sell next month. You never know," the coach explains. "That's why the best approach is consistent marketing over the long haul."

Taking the long-haul approach requires a consistently powerful message, delivered in a package that's convenient for the customers. Every time your name, logo, and photo show up in their email inbox, for example, it shows them that you are a professional. It ingrains your image on their psyche. At the time, they may not even be thinking about calling a real estate agent to list their home, but that doesn't matter. What matters is that you're becoming their agent of choice <u>before</u> they even need your services.

Assessing the Competition

One of the first things any good business owner does before getting into business is to assess the competition. That's because in order to succeed in the marketplace, you simply must know "what else is out there," and how you can stand head and shoulders above the rest and leverage your individual strengths to your advantage. The latter is particularly relevant for real estate agents, who "cooperate" with other agents in the marketplace to get deals closed.

Ultimately, your own marketing plan must meet a customer need in a way that's somehow better than your competition. Here are the key issues to consider during this assessment process:

- Who your competitors are, where they're located, how long they've been in the business and (if possible) just how successful they've been in the market over the last 12 to 24 months
- Your competitors' strengths and weaknesses
- An idea of what your competitors are planning to do next (keeping up with trade journals and participating in activities at your local trade association are good ways to stay in the loop)
- Your competitors' spending trends

Going a step further, new businesses should also do a thorough competitive analysis prior to opening their doors, in an effort to truly understand the competitive nature of the business and where they stand in the marketplace. Here are the six points that should be covered in the competitive analysis:

1. Who are your five nearest direct competitors?
2. Who are your indirect competitors?
3. Is their business growing, steady, or declining?
4. What can you learn from their operations or from their advertising efforts?
5. What are their strengths and weaknesses?
6. How does their product or service differ from yours?

Start a file on each of your competitors that includes advertising, promotional materials, and pricing strategies. Review these files periodically, determining how often they advertise, sponsor promotions, and offer discounts to their customers. Study the copy used in the advertising and promotional materials, as well as their sales strategies.

If you're unsure of where to go for some of this information, check out the following resources:

- Web and social: These are obvious and powerful tools for finding information on virtually anything you want to know. A great source of "competitive intelligence" on your market, competitors, and customers, the web as a whole and social networking sites are both great resources for new agents.
- Personal visits: Visit your competitors' locations if possible. Observe how employees interact with customers. What do their premises look like? How are their services marketed and priced?
- Talk to customers: You're probably in regular contact with customers and prospects, but so are your competitors. To learn what your customers and prospects are saying about your competitors, just ask them.
- Competitors' ads, websites, and social media: Look carefully at competitors' ads, websites, Facebooks, Twitters, and Active Rain accounts to learn about their target audiences, market positions, product features, and benefits, prices, etc.
- Speeches or presentations: Attend speeches or presentations that your competitors are participating in.
- Trade show displays: View your competitor's display from a potential customer's point of view. What does their display say about the company? Observing which specific trade shows or industry events competitors attend provides information on their marketing strategy and target market.
- Written sources, such as:
  - General business publications
  - Marketing and advertising publications

- Local newspapers and business journals
- Industry and trade association publications
- Industry research and surveys

Once you've gathered the pertinent information, plug it into the following competitive analysis:

- Names of competitors: List all of your current competitors and research any that might enter the market during the next year.
- Summary of each competitor's products: This should include location, quality, advertising, staff, distribution methods, promotional strategies, customer service, etc.
- Competitors' strengths and weaknesses: List their strengths and weaknesses from the customer's viewpoint. State how you will capitalize on their weaknesses and meet the challenges represented by their strengths.
- Competitors' strategies and objectives: Check out annual reports, websites, social media pages, and past articles in publications (both online and offline).
- Strength of the market: Is the market for your product growing sufficiently so there are enough customers for all market players?

Once completed, this exercise should provide you with a clear idea of what you're up against in the industry, gaps in the market that are aching to be filled by a good agent and exactly how you can create a business that stands heads and shoulders above the competition. This competitive intelligence will also help you develop your own value proposition. For example, you might find that there's a "gap" in your market for certain buyer demographics, a dearth of agents specializing in luxury properties, or a market niche that's right up your alley (i.e., working with millennial clients because you are one yourself, or catering to older homeowners who want to downsize).

Creating Your Plan

Becoming top of mind in a competitive marketplace starts with a good marketing plan that covers—at minimum—the following components. Many of these issues are typically covered in the "market analysis" section of a standard business plan:

- **An overview of your target market:** Here's where you'll dig down and find out the nitty-gritty details of your market. Getting this done before you start transacting business is optimal (but if you're already working, by all means start now). With this information at hand, you'll be able to better determine exactly where your services fit into the market, or what you'll need to do to tweak your plan to better serve that market's needs. When completing this section, be sure to include the following:
  - Current population and population growth
  - Number of homes, and number of homes constructed annually
  - Demographics of your customer base (generally available from your city's economic development departments or online at the Bureau of Labor Statistics (www.bls.gov) and related sources):
    - Are they male or female?
    - Are they single, or do they have families?
    - What race and ethnic backgrounds are most prominent in my area?
    - How old are my primary, secondary, and tertiary client bases? (For example, Baby Boomers, empty nesters have different housing needs than Millennial homebuyers).
    - Where do these potential clients work and what are their annual average incomes?
- **An outline of your service strategy:** In this section you'll describe in as much detail as possible how your service differs

from that of your competitors (who include not only agents working for another brokerage, but also those agents sitting on either side of you in the office). When developing this strategy, ask yourself the following questions:

- Which service offerings are most important to my customers? (Do they need help with the entire real estate transaction, for example, or are they well-versed in the process and simply in need of fee-based services like holding open houses and showing their homes to prospective buyers?)
- Are customers willing to pay a premium for these services, and will they continue paying a premium in exchange for my services in this realm? (Be sure to factor in the dynamic qualities of a real estate market. Realize that it is indeed cyclical in nature and dependent on a number of different economic factors, including interest rates, home value appreciation, and stock market performance.)
- What will the customer value over the long-term, and how can I center my services on these wants and needs? (Repeat customers and the referrals that they generate are worth their weight in gold.)
- Why would a customer switch to my services? (Consider, for example, someone who may have been working with an agent who is a close friend or relative of theirs.)
- How will I retain customers so that they won't stray to another agent in the future? (Many agents believe in using a combination of email, social media, mobile marketing, and snail/direct mail to "reach out" to past clients at least once a month, for instance.)
- What technological tools (texting, social networking, virtual conferencing, etc.) can I employ to best serve my target customer base?

- What type of ongoing support will I provide to customers to make sure they come back to me when it's time to buy or sell?
- **Details on your pricing approach:** What you jot down for this section is highly dependent on what type of broker you've chosen to hang your license with. Commissions are negotiable, according to real estate license law, but it's the generally the broker who establishes a "set point" that the agents use in the office. There are exceptions to the rule, of course, but for the most part agents offer their services at 5 to 7 percent of the sales price, depending on geographic location. You'll need to look around in your own market and talk to the broker about your own pricing approach, since policies can include:
  - **A full-service broker:** Generally charges between 5 and 7 percent of the sales price, with the total amount divided between the agent and the broker (on a pre-determined scale that differs from broker to broker). It's important to note that commissions are negotiable, and that some of the more established full-service brokers include Coldwell Banker, Century 21 and Keller Williams.
  - **A full-service, 100 percent broker:** These companies charge the same market rates, but 100 percent (or close to it) of the commission goes to the agent. This gives the agent a bit more leeway in determining their price, though most stick to the going rate in the market unless the situation warrants a different arrangement. RE/MAX is a good example of this type of brokerage.
  - **A discount, online, or flat-fee broker:** Working virtually or online, these firms have their own set pricing strategies that range from 2 percent commissions to flat fee. If you've hung your license at one of these shops, your broker will provide the details you need to fill in this pricing section of your marketing plan.

- **A broker that offers menu options:** This is a hybrid between a full-service and discount broker, the latter of which came to be when someone realized that not all consumers need or want full service from their agents. With menu options, an agent offers their services in exchange for a flat fee, such as $2,000 to handle several open houses or $2,500 to draw up contracts for the sale. Brokers and agents generally work out the details between one another before offering such services.

- **Your advertising and promotion plans:** Getting your name and face out into the public—which will eventually become your customer base—is critical for new agents, particularly those who come into the business without an established "sphere of influence" (or, group of people who are ready and willing to buy and sell homes, or that will point customers in your direction). Here are some key questions to consider when completing this important section of your marketing plan:

  - **What are the best, most affordable ways that I can start promoting my business right now?** The web has really leveled the playing field for new agents who can "go the extra mile" online and present themselves in a desirable light without needing decades of experience under their belts.

  - **What resources do I have at my avail that will cost little to reach?** Business clubs, chambers of commerce, and networking meetings are a good starting point. Because nearly 100 percent of homebuyers start their home searches online now, web-based leads are a good option for new agents that don't have an immediate sphere of influence to tap into. Conversation rates tend to be low on online leads, but if you can manage the volume and respond quickly (30 seconds or less, in some cases), this can be a good way to start the foundation for your successful career.

- **How can I get free publicity?** Local daily and weekly newspapers, blogs, online publications, and other media outlets frequently run stories on successful businesspeople. Since your audience will probably be mainly local (usually the norm, unless you're in a market where second home buyers are most prevalent), this is a perfect way to raise awareness of your business.
- **Can I sponsor teams, events, or programs?** Little League teams, soccer clubs, and other community programs are always on the lookout for sponsors. Where I live, a $500 donation to our local soccer club yields the donor a large, banner-size ad on the fence at a club. This is the spot where hundreds of parents and children spend their weekends and weekday evenings in the fall and winter months.

- **Your overall sales strategy:** In this section you'll tie together all of the other components mentioned above into one, succinct description of your firm's sales strategy. New agents can stick to the basics in this section, but existing agents who are looking to grow their firms want to go further. Basically, you'll want to look at what you (and any of your employees or assistants) are going to do to boost your firm's sales, and how you're going to manage growth once it becomes too much for one person to handle. The answers to the following questions will help you fill this section:
  - How many salespeople do I need (other than myself) right now?
  - How many will I need one year from now, should I reach my sales goals over the next 12 months?
  - What kind of customer support do I need to offer, and how does this level of customer service affect my overall sales?
  - When the time comes, will I hire employees or can I outsource some of these services to a virtual assistant? (Keep an

eye on state licensing laws, as most have set forth guidelines governing the work of licensed vs. unlicensed assistants)
- What other sales support do I need to have in place in order to reach my financial and life goals?

- **Approximate marketing budget:** One of the most challenging tasks facing a small business owner is just how much money to invest in marketing and advertising themselves and their companies to the world. Spend too much and you risk going into the red financially. Spend too little and what you spent will be for naught, since customers won't know that you exist. In this section, you'll review your marketing needs vs. your financial resources and decide just how much money to allocate on a weekly or monthly basis for marketing. Remember that this will be a moving target, since a few good commission checks can free up extra cash for advertising, while coming up short can find you holding back on the purse strings for a couple of weeks. The key is to deliver a consistent, steady message to the public about your services and do it in a manner that's both affordable and effective.

There's no specific formula for developing a marketing budget, though most firms use a basic "percentage of sales" approach. According to Real Trends, 53 percent of real estate professionals spent less than $5,000 annually on marketing, including both online and offline avenues. However, it says that one in eight agents spent more than $20,000 annually on marketing, with the top 3 percent of earners spending more than $80,000.

"I invest 10 to 15 percent of my annual GCI [gross commissionable income] into marketing and 80 percent of that investment is into online channels, including my website, search engine optimization, and pay per click advertising," one top-selling agent told Real Trends. "As a result of this investment, approximately 50 percent of my clients find me online, although we still invest in traditional newspaper and magazine marketing too."

The good news is that digital marketing has made advertising yourself and your listings much more affordable. The not-so-good news is that the online world is cluttered with agents who are doing the same thing that you are! As a rule of thumb, you can use these estimates to develop your marketing budget:

- First year: 20–30 percent of projected sales
- Second year: 10–15 percent of projected sales
- Third year and beyond: 5–10 percent of projected sales

Keep in mind that this is a formula that applies to all businesses, and that real estate by nature is a highly advertising-intensive industry that has higher-than-usual advertising needs.

Real Estate Specific

When drafting your marketing plan, be sure to include real estate-specific points that will help you get a handle not only on your budget, but also on the effectiveness of your methods and choices. That way, the next time a salesperson from a real estate or homes-related magazine or website tries to sell your advertising, you'll be able to quickly determine whether or not the investment is worth your time, energy, and money. The first step is to objectively review your marketing strategies from the consumer's points of view. "Agents don't inherently take this step," says one real estate coach. Instead, they come up with generalizations like:

"If I'm a better agent than the one who sold me my house, then I'll be able to do a better job."

Or:

"I'm going to build my marketing around service."

Understand that such statements are too general, and that most consumers don't actually discern between agents in terms of experience (unless they're already acquainted with them, or have worked with them in the past). Instead, they tend to lump all licensed agents (including those who are members of the national, state, and regional REALTOR associations) into one category, assuming that because these agents are licensed they must be adequately qualified and knowledgeable.

To sharpen up your own message, use your marketing plans to build your positioning or "point of difference," in the market. Do this by asking yourself the following questions:

- What is my target market (outlined above in the first section of your marketing plan) buying right now?
- What needs and wants are driving their purchasing decisions?
- Knowing these needs, wants, and habits, what can I provide to these customers that no other agent can?
- How can I maximize these differentiations in the marketplace in an effective, affordable manner?
- What are my own strengths and weaknesses, and how can I capitalize on the strengths and minimize the weaknesses when I'm working in the market?

"Build your positioning on your point of difference," says one seasoned real estate coach. "If you take the time to do this, you'll have a leg up on the competition because most agents don't ever analyze their own strengths and weaknesses. Instead, they select methods that are inherently marketing-challenged to start with."

The next step is to analyze customer response—or, exactly how your potential or current customers are responding to your marketing methods. If you find that your outgoing personality helps you win friends and influence people, for example, then you'll want to put that personality trait to good use while you're out in the field selling homes. If, on the other hand, customers seem to respond better to your low-pressure, conservative type of personality, then use your character to communicate with customers in a manner that makes them both comfortable and responsive.

Find something in your personality that you can build your marketing plan on, and make sure your marketing materials reflect those traits and values. Because each individual agent is different, and because real estate is a fragmented industry where many different types of business models are currently in use, it's difficult to pinpoint even the most basic of marketing strategies without using a hypothetical example as a guide. Here are two very different "farm area" examples that illustrate a few key real estate-specific marketing strategies.

Example #1:

- **Farm area:** Seacliff Estates
- **Number of Homes:** 1,500
- **Media options for this farm area:** A neighborhood social site (like NextDoor) that covers the area, plus 14,000 other homes that you're <u>not</u> trying to reach. Direct mail and door-to-door farming are other good approaches for agents looking to reach out to those homeowners.

Example #2:

- **Farm area:** Pinewood Forest
- **Number of homes:** 10,000
- **Media options for this farm area:** A neighborhood newspaper that covers the area, Facebook ads, and a few cable television options and strategically placed billboards. In this market, the agent has more ways to reach out to a wider audience.

Understand that neither option is better or worse than the other, and that this simply shows the difference between two marketing plans for two different agents. The agent working in a small town where direct mail is the best choice, for example, isn't necessarily going to do better than the agent who has access to television and billboards to reach out to the audience. That's because the latter may be working in a market where competition for listings and buyers is stiff. It's simply a matter of geography, and personal choice. The key is to understand the audience and your place in the market. You then need to leverage your strengths and competitive advantages to get out there and start working with this group.

Getting Affordable

Flip through your favorite online or offline real estate magazines and you'll see a plethora of multi-color ads showcasing homes and the agents that have them listed for sale. Grab a home magazine off the "free" publication pile and you'll get an eyeful of full-page and multi-page ads of the same nature. On the Internet, a quick search for agents in your area will reveal a number of elaborate websites equipped with virtual tours and listing and pricing data. The same agents are probably using Instagram, Facebook, and Snapchat to let the world know about their services.

Let's face it, marketing and advertising isn't cheap, nor is it always effective. New agents in particular take a gamble when plunking down cash in exchange for a new marketing method, since most lack the benchmarks or historical data needed to make comparisons. And while the agents in your office can be a good source of feedback, one agent's negative feedback concerning the use of "just listed" or "just sold" postcards doesn't necessarily mean that such direct mail pieces will not work for you.

"Unfortunately, agents are always looking for generalizations," says the real estate coach. "But generalizations are not always available, nor are they always accurate." When figuring a marketing budget, for example, he says most experts agree that an agent should allocate 30 percent of his projected, first-year's gross sales to marketing. The number then tails off as the agent progresses in the business. For example:

- First year's projected sales: $100,000
- First year's marketing budget: $30,000 a year or $2,500 per month (at 30 percent)
- Second year's projected sales: $150,000
- Second year's marketing budget: $22,500 a year or $1875 per month (at 15 percent)

Too often, agents skimp on marketing, particularly during those first couple of "lean" years. Using the formula above, they underestimate their annual sales and end up spending far too little money to get their companies rolling. The problem is if you have no sales and you spend 15 percent, you end up with nothing. This is not a situation that you want to be in as either a new or existing agent.

The good news for agents on a budget is that there are some great marketing tactics out there that don't cost a fortune. Here are some starter ideas to use right now to expand your client base and spread the word about your real estate service offerings:

- **Get out of your office and start talking to people:** Real estate is very much a "word of mouth" industry, where good news travels fast and bad news travels even faster. Agents tend to be a tightly networked group of individuals who seem to "know everyone." For a spot on that A-list, get out into the community and start schmoozing with people. Spread the word about your business to everyone you meet and hand out business cards, connect on social media sites, and sign up for Yahoo and Google business pages. Tell everyone that you're a real estate agent. I once knew an agent who got most of her clients—either directly, or by referral—from the parents she mingled with on a daily basis at her daughter's elementary school. Another one got the bulk of her new customers at the dog park, and yet another is a former physical therapist who works with a high number of professional athletes (as clients) thanks to his previous career.

- **Seek out free publicity opportunities:** As mentioned earlier in this chapter, media outlets are always looking for successful businesspeople to feature in their publications or shows. Since real estate agents tend to be active in their communities, consider associating yourself with a local event, then alert media to the event and your availability for interviews. One successful agent in New York, for example, prides himself on being a prominent figure in the community. He's a patron of the arts. He's sponsored concerts, served on various boards of directors and volunteered his time to various associations.

- **Ask for referrals:** The average agent doesn't properly educate her clients early enough to start thinking about giving her referrals. When meeting a potential client for the first time, for example, one agent tells them that she wants to work with people on a win-win basis. She says to them, "If at the end of buying or selling your home you feel I have taken good care of you and given you great value, will you be willing to commit to referring me at least two people during the following 12 months?" She then reinforces that commitment throughout the transaction so that her clients <u>expect</u> to send her referrals. Other ways to ensure referrals include: sending out thank you notes for a referral that's received and using a database to track both customers and the referrals.

- **Use email:** Email is a flexible, cost-effective, and easy way to reach out to customers on their own terms. A great method of staying in touch with past clients, via short newsletters, updates, new listing announcements, and other tools, email also helps you drive traffic to your website, reach a broad geographic audience, and stay in frequent contact with your customers and prospects. Email marketing allows you to market your services and establish your expertise with your audience (just be sure to comply with anti-spam rules when doing so).

- **Think outside of the box:** Don't be afraid to check out what people in other industries are doing and then adapt those tools and strategies in your business. Think about the little details that will get attention. For example, if you have a buyer who is chomping at the bit for a home in a certain neighborhood where no homes are currently on the market, why not make up a targeted postcard offering to introduce your buyer to a potential seller in that neighborhood? On the Fourth of July, why not go out to your farm area and put U.S. flags in the ground at each home, and include a business card or message identifying you as the agent of choice for that particular area? Get creative and have some fun thinking outside of the box.

For Existing Agents

The bulk of this chapter is geared to the new agent who needs a concept-to-completion marketing plan. But that doesn't mean marketing plans are only for the new and uninitiated. All agents, no matter what level of success they've achieved, need a solid marketing plan in order to learn what works, what doesn't, what needs to be tweaked, and what should be thrown out the window.

Write your marketing plan down and review it quarterly and annually, with the latter comprising a more thorough, intensive look at what's working and what's not. Should a plan be changed daily? Absolutely not, since most marketing efforts take time to mature and produce results. However, if your instincts are telling you that a certain strategy (say, a revamped website or a better social media strategy) isn't producing results, then you'll definitely want to pare down your investment in that area.

One sure sign that your marketing plan needs tweaking is a stagnating business, particularly in a market where your competitors seem to be doing just fine. "If you're not growing at 5 or 10 percent a year, then something is eroding your client base," says the real estate coach. "There should be a steady, upward trend in sales. If there isn't, then it's time to look at your overall business plan and marketing plan to pinpoint the problem."

During this exercise, look at the key points:

- How much of my business is coming from new clients?
- How much comes from past clients?
- How much is coming from referral clients?

If the percentage is heavily weighted on past clients, for example, it could signal the need for better marketing strategies to drum up new business. If your new business pipeline is full but referrals are nonexistent, then it's time to put more effort into "asking for the referral" rather than just assuming that someone will point a customer in your direction.

By going through this review process on a quarterly basis (reviewing last quarter and comparing it to the same period in the prior year, if possible) and annual basis (looking at the past 12 months, and contrasting that against the previous 12 months, if those numbers are available), you'll know exactly what you need to do to reach your firm's financial goals.

It's all part of good planning. "Planning is the best investment an agent will ever make," the real estate coach concludes. "Learning to work 'on' your business instead of 'in' your business is critical. It takes you from being trapped by your business to actually managing a company that you can be happy with, and that will help you achieve your goals."

6 Unique Way to Find Customers for Your Real Estate Business

For years I've written for a number of state REALTOR magazines, including Texas REALTOR, RE Magazine (Washington), Bay State REALTOR, and Florida Realtor. In this role, I've interviewed hundreds of agents and brokers about the best ways to market and grow a real estate business. Here are some of their best ideas for drumming up new business and standing out from your competitors:

1. **Establish your own business networking group.** As a long-time Business Networking International (BNI) member, David Chirico knew the ins and outs of running a successful networking group. When he had an issue with a fellow member and left BNI in 2007, Chirico established the Best of the Best Networking Group and attracted 90 members within 12 months. He now runs six different organizations whose members—each of which represents a different profession—meet on a weekly basis to network with one another. Chirico invested about $50,000 in the marketing approach (most of it to cover an automated website that even tracks referrals shared via cell phone among members) and estimates that it takes about 10 hours a week to run it. In return, Chirico says he's connected with buyers, sell-

ers, and owners of rental property through the group. Intent on turning Best of the Best into a national organization, Chirico says the group also makes him more recognizable in the community and shows his "commitment to helping other business professionals achieve their own goals."

2. **Start your own radio show.** Every Saturday from 2–3pm Brandon Rimes can be found educating, enlightening, and inspiring Tampa's 1250 WHNZ listeners about real estate, mortgage, and credit. Using the Real Estate Quarterback Show as a conduit, he invites local mayors, politicians, nonprofit leaders, and local business owners to join him on the air for an hour every week to discuss topics like mortgage rates, flood insurance, and the government shutdown. A former University of South Florida football player, Rimes invested an undisclosed sum (sponsorships and advertising can be used to offset the costs) in a one-year contract to host the show, which requires several hours of time every week for preparation and planning. Rimes says his goal is to position himself as a leader in Tampa Bay's real estate market and also to increase his "real estate quarterback" brand recognition. He can trace several closed deals and referrals to the show and says the marketing effort has also exposed him to new potential business partnerships and synergies. "The show has helped me grow my network," says Rimes, "serve as a consumer advocate, and get involved with new projects like area home shows."

3. **Set up a community movie night.** Once a month Jack Mancini rolls his moving van to a central location in his subdivision, sets up a projector and receiver, pops in a DVD, fires up a high-end popcorn machine, and waits for roughly 100 parents and children to gather around for movie night. Wrapped in an advertisement, the van serves multiple purposes as a moving vehicle for buyers and sellers to use, a projection screen for the movies, and a "wrapped" billboard for his real estate business. Mancini, who invested under $1,000 in the marketing idea

and spends about an hour a month on setup and breakdown, netted five new deals (about $25,000 in commissions) from the initiative in one year. He uses the Stoneybrook in Estero newsletter to advertise the event and says he'd like to take the concept out into other communities in the area. "People really seem to love it," says Mancini, "and respond well to it, both in terms of the steady attendance and through the new business opportunities I've gotten out of it."

4. **Invest in pay-per-click advertising.** Mitch Ribak says many of his team's deals can be traced back to the $10,000 per month that he invests in pay-per-click (PPC) advertising on Google and Facebook—the latter of which consumes a lesser portion of that budget but yields solid results. "The cool thing about Facebook PPC is that you can really hone in on your target market," says Ribak, who recently used the strategy to test out the response for several evaluation websites. Using Facebook, he can zero in on users who are within a certain age bracket, working for an organization like NASA or Harris, or interested in home warranties. The upside of PPC on Facebook versus Google, says Ribak, is that it costs less because you only pay when someone actually "clicks." The downside, he adds, is that fewer people click on the ads (due to the more targeted nature of the marketing effort). It takes about a month to develop and tweak an effective PPC campaign, according to Ribak, who has also invested considerably in an effective online lead conversion solution. "We've automated the entire lead process—from capture to conversion," says Ribak. "That's where the real work—and the payoff—on PCC comes in."

5. **Wear a REALTOR pin.** As a corporate trainer, Denise Oyler knows that most nascent real estate agents don't have huge marketing budgets. In fact, some of them have minimal resources at their avail and a need for new clients quickly. Oyler, who specializes in working with newly-licensed agents, says the good news is that building a brand doesn't have to cost and arm and a

leg. For example, simply wearing a REALTOR pin can lead to a slew of new business. "This is a simple strategy that costs literally no money at all," says Oyler, who wears her own REALTOR pin not only on her clothing, but also on her yoga mat strap. While visiting her mother in the hospital recently, Oyler says two different doctors who noticed the pin stopped her in the hallway and asked about available properties in the area. And don't forget the dog park. "Take your dog—or, borrow one—out to the pet park," says Oyler, who affixes her REALTOR pin to her pet's collar before sending Fido out to corral around with the other dogs. Comments like, "My gosh puppy, do you sell real estate?" from other pet owners can quickly evolve into conversations about buying and selling properties.

CHAPTER FOUR
Treat it Like a Business

Just because real estate agents have desks, workspaces, on-the-job training, and guidance from a broker or manager, it doesn't mean they can afford to act like employees. Real estate may feel like a "job," says one successful agent, "but it's really anything but." In real estate since 1989, this agent sells about $8 million+ in properties each year and says she wishes someone had informed her of her small-business owner status a lot earlier in her career.

"This is no sales job," says the agent. "You have to treat it as if you were self-employed, and like you are the CEO of your own company. It took me 10 years to realize that I was a business owner, and not just someone who was driving around selling homes." Once she did catch on, she incorporated her business and got a grip on her expenses, instead of spending commission checks freely as they came in.

These days, the agent cuts herself a regular paycheck, pays payroll taxes monthly, allocates a portion of her business' income for estimated tax payments and tracks expenditures carefully—just like any responsible business owner would. As a result, she says she has a good handle on her company's revenues and expenditures, knows how profitable her business is, allocates a certain percentage of revenues to marketing and is much better prepared when tax time rolls around.

It's *Not* a Job

According to one California-based real estate coach, the biggest mistake that agents make is that they treat their new career like a job, rather than a business. Unfortunately, since the majority of them work on commissions, that kind of mistake can get pretty costly, pretty quickly.

"Agents know that they're independent contractors, but they still operate as if they had jobs," he points out. "That kills most agents' chances for success because no matter how many hours they put in, they won't get paid unless they actually perform, and sell homes." The fact that real estate is a time-consuming, all-encompassing type of "job" doesn't help either. Agents can literally spend all day answering phone calls, driving through neighborhoods, searching the MLS for new and expired listings, and pressing the flesh with their contact base—all without generating any immediate income.

"So many agents struggle with that mentally, and never quite grasp the fact that just because you put in the time, doesn't mean you're going to make money," says the coach, who advises all agents to create a business plan to avoid getting sidetracked by mundane, day-to-day tasks that don't generate income. "Creating a business plan will significantly increase the odds of succeeding in this business."

Business Sense

The correlation between thinking like a business owner and acting like a real estate agent is clear, but how does one go about adopting that mindset? Start by asking yourself these 20 pertinent questions that any new entrepreneur should consider before opening up a new business:

1. Am I a hard worker?
2. Am I self-motivated?
3. Am I an optimist and a risk taker, like most successful business owners are?

4. Do I have the self-starter determination to get this business going, and the discipline and dedication to keep it on track?
5. Do I take responsibility for my own actions?
6. Am I a good problem solver?
7. Am I organized?
8. Do I have the stamina and desire to put in long hours?
9. Am I willing to work weekends and evenings, when most homebuyers are out looking at houses?
10. Do I consider ethics and honesty to be important ingredients for a successful career in business?
11. Am I usually able to come up with more than one way to solve a problem?
12. Can I live on my savings and/or my partner's income for at least six to 12 months while I build this business?
13. Will my family and friends support my efforts?
14. Am I business savvy, or do I have a colleague or friend who can help me through the critical first few stages of business?
15. Am I prepared to make sacrifices in my family life and take a cut in pay to succeed in business?
16. Am I the kind of person that once I decide to do something I'll do it and nothing can stop me?
17. When I begin a task, do I set clear goals and objectives for myself?
18. When I've done a good job, am I satisfied in knowing personally that the job has been done?
19. After a severe setback in a project, am I able to pick up the pieces and start over again?
20. Do I enjoy working on projects that I know will take a long time to complete successfully?

Don't worry if you didn't answer a resounding "yes" to every one of these questions, but if you were negative on five or more points, you may want to reconsider the "small business" aspect of being a real estate agent. It's truly an entrepreneurial endeavor, particularly for the first two to three years, and a big undertaking that is not for the faint of heart. The sooner you come to grips with this reality, the better off you'll be. That means putting in long hours, operating on a lean and often fluctuating income, striving to find and keep customers, and even spinning your wheels a bit as you figure what strategies work best, and ultimately reap the rewards of your sweat equity.

One Florida-based CPA says being self-employed requires a 180-degree switch in viewpoint, particularly if the agent hails from a 9–5-job setting. "An employee is rewarded for showing up every day, interacting pleasantly with peers and clients, and doing his or her assigned tasks," she states. "He or she has little direct stake in the results achieved or concern about net profits or making final management decisions." Agents, on the other hand, are largely responsible for their own successes or failures. Employee behavior will generate only marginal income, she points out, and a lack of management perspective can result in long hours, little reward, and burnout.

To avoid such issues in your own real estate career, you'll need to organize your business approach. Start your own organizational journey with these seven easy steps:

1. Start at square one, like any new business owner would. Instead of jumping right into selling homes, spend time planning, assessing, and researching before "opening your doors."
2. Identify what you're selling, to whom, and how you'll go about doing that. (See Chapter Three, Marketing).
3. Pick a specialty and stick with it. "No one should be a 'threshold' agent (i.e., where anyone who walks across the agent's "threshold" qualifies as a client.)," says the CPA. "Just like Bloomingdales deals on the higher end of the retail market, its marketing matches the company's niche customers and

its environment is specifically designed for a specific crowd. Agents should specialize too."

4. Attend local SDBC (Small Business Development Center) seminars to learn how to start your own business, develop a business plan, and create a marketing strategy. (A list of offices is online here: https://americassbdc.org/) Although the focus will be on typical retail and service businesses, real estate professionals should reword the examples to fit their own focus.

5. Envision your business. Books like SYOB: Start Your Own Business and Starting a Business All-in-One for Dummies can help you with some of the more difficult aspects of starting a business. Check out Amazon for a full listing of business startup guides.

6. Track income and expenses. Use a program like QuickBooks® Basic Accounting software and review monthly financial statements. Start this practice early and you'll have the right systems in place when your real estate business starts generating income.

7. Name your business. Create a logo or identifying tag line, just as any new business would. In some states due to licensing regulations, a business name may be for the agent's internal use only and not shared with the public. Check with your state's real estate commission for more information on this topic.

Existing agents who need a refresher course on business ownership should take the same steps outlined above. "No matter what stage of the game they're at, agents should revamp their internal image from 'real estate agent' to 'small business owner,'" says the CPA. "The key is to embrace this new concept by following the steps recommended for all new business startups."

Cash is King

When you start thinking like a small business owner, finances will probably consume a good portion of your "leftover" time (i.e., the time that's not spent working with buyers and sellers). That's because for the small business owner, cash flow is king. Without it, computers and devices can't be purchased, employees can't be paid and business can't be conducted. As the lifeblood of any company, cash flow includes currency, checks on hand, and bank deposits. Cash equivalents are short-term, temporary investments like treasury bills, certificates of deposit, or commercial paper that can be quickly and easily converted into cash.

Armed with cash, a business can pay bills, repay loans, make investments, and provide goods and services to its customers. Cash also plays a critical role in generating even more cash when higher profits start to roll in. The fundamentals of cash flow seem simple enough, but the real question is: how does a small business owner go about creating an accurate picture of the operation's cash flow?

First, create a cash flow statement that clearly documents the movement of cash in and out of your company in any given year. A cash flow statement reports a business' sources and uses of cash along with the beginning and ending values for cash and cash equivalents each year. It also includes the combined total change in cash and cash equivalents from all sources and uses of cash.

There are generally two methods for calculating cash flow from operating activities: indirect and direct.

Indirect Method:
Popular because of its relative simplicity, the indirect method starts with a figure for net income (from your income statement) and helps you adjust this accrual amount for any items that do not affect cash flow.

There are three basic types of adjustments:
- Revenues and expenses that do not involve cash inflows or outflows (i.e., cost allocations such as depreciation and amortization).

- Gains and losses on events reported in other sections of the statement of cash flows.
- Conversions of current operating assets and liabilities from the accrual to the cash basis.

Direct Method:
The direct method, although less popular, is favored by many financial managers because it reports the source of cash inflows and outflows directly, without the potentially confusing adjustments to net income.

Instead of starting with a reported net income, the direct method analyzes the various types of operating activities and calculates the total cash flow created by each one. Before beginning the direct method, all accrual accounts must first be converted to a cash figure.

Cash Flow Statements are broken down into three sections: operating activities, investing activities, and financing activities. Here's a quick breakdown of each (for more in-depth coverage be sure to talk to your accountant):

Operating activities
Operating activities (all transactions and events that normally enter into the determination of operating income) include cash receipts from selling goods or providing services, as well as income from items such as interest and dividends. Operating activities also include your cash payments such as inventory, payroll, taxes, interest, utilities, and rent.

The net amount of cash provided (or used) by operating activities is the key figure on a statement of cash flows.

Cash receipts include:
- Sale of goods or services
- Interest revenue
- Dividend revenue

Cash payments include:
- Inventory purchases

- Payroll
- Taxes
- Interest expense
- Other (utilities, rent, etc.)

Note: While cash inflows from interest or dividends could be considered investing or financing activities, the Financial Accounting Standards Board classifies them as operating activities.

Investing activities

Investing activities include transactions and events involving the purchase and sale of securities (excluding cash equivalents), land, buildings, equipment, and other assets not generally held for resale. It also covers the making and collecting of loans. Investing activities are not classified as operating activities because they have an indirect relationship to the central, ongoing operation of your business (usually the sale of goods or services).

Cash receipts include:

- Sale of plant assets
- Sale of a business segment
- Sale of investments in equity securities of other entities or debt securities (other than cash equivalents)
- Collection of principal on loans made to other entities

Cash payments include:

- Purchase of plant assets
- Purchase of equity securities of other entities or debt securities (other than cash equivalents)
- Loans to other entities

Financing activities

All financing activities deal with the flow of cash to or from the business owners (equity financing) and creditors (debt financing). For example, cash proceeds from issuing capital stock or bonds would be classified under financing activities. Likewise, payments to repurchase stock (treasury stock) or to retire bonds and the payment of dividends are financing activities as well.

Cash receipts include:

- Issuance of own stock
- Borrowing (bonds, notes, mortgages, etc.)

Cash payments include:

- Dividends to stockholders
- Repaying principal amounts borrowed
- Repurchasing business' own stock (treasury stock)

Once you've created a cash flow statement for your company, you'll have a much better understanding of your firm's financial position and be able to make more informed decisions regarding its future. A cash flow statement is important to your business because it can be used to assess the timing and the amount and predictability of future cash flows. It can be the basis for budgeting—a very important issue in the real estate industry, where commission checks can be spaced out throughout the year—and help answer questions like: Where did the money come from? Where was it spent and why?

To Incorporate or Not?

One way to really start feeling like a small business owner is by incorporating your business, although not all new agents will want to take this step fresh out of real estate school. Once the commissions start rolling in, however, you may want to join the ranks of business owners that have shed their sole proprietorships in favor of corporations.

One small business consultant for the National Association for the Self-Employed (NASE) says issues surrounding incorporation are a hot topic for his group's many members. "It's a major issue, and the number one or number two question that our Shop Talk consultants work through with small business owners," he says. "I'd venture to say incorporating is the most predominant issue for micro and small businesses."

Business owners are generally most concerned with which legal entity to select, afraid that the incorrect choice may hurt their companies. Basic choices include the partnership, the LLC, the C Corp. (a traditional corporation) and the S Corp. Chartered by the state in which it is headquartered, the corporation is considered by law to be a unique entity, separate and apart from those who own it, according to the U.S. Small Business Administration.

A corporation can be taxed and sued, and can enter into contractual agreements. The owners of a corporation are its shareholders who elect a board of directors to oversee the major policies and decisions. The corporation has a life of its own and does not dissolve when ownership changes. The S Corp. is a tax election that enables the shareholder to treat the earnings and profits as distributions and have them pass thru directly to their personal tax returns. The shareholders (if working for the company, and if there is a profit) must pay themselves and must meet standards of "reasonable compensation."

Another option is the Limited Liability Company (LLC). Defined as a hybrid business structure, the LLC is designed to provide the limited liability features of a corporation and the tax efficiencies and operational flexibility of a partnership, though formation is more complex and formal than that of a general partnership.

To get more information about business incorporation, visit the U.S. Small Business Administration Website at (www.sba.gov) or do a Google search. Do this before making your selection and/or investing any money in the process. Steer clear of companies making claims like, "Incorporate in Delaware or Nevada for $300," as such groups aren't credible and can lead to major headaches for the business owner. "Do your homework," says the small business consultant. "Get some professional guidance, research the options, and then select the entity that fits well with your own business goals and aspirations."

And remember that incorporating is more than just filing paperwork. Agents should always seek help from a small business CPA or attorney, who will probably charge about $500 to $1500 for professional assistance provided throughout the process. There are also online companies like LegalZoom that offer this service, so it just depends on how much handholding and support you need during the process. Thoroughly research the different entities, because in some cases an LLC (limited liability company) may be a better choice than a corporation. Finally, check with your state real estate licensing agency to see if it allows individual agents to incorporate.

Here's a quick look at the pros and cons of incorporating your real estate business:

- Benefits:
    - Opportunity to select subchapter S corporate tax treatment, which can lower an agent's cost of Social Security and Medicare tax.
    - Liability protection from acts of competently-managed employees.
    - Easier to qualify for corporate discounts.
    - Easier to qualify for contractor credit cards offered by building supply companies like Home Depot and Lowe's.
    - Easier to qualify for credit cards offered by office retailers like Staples.
    - Helps solidify the agent's self-image as a small business owner.

- Downfalls:
    - Additional annual cost of having a corporate tax return prepared (usually $500 to $1000, with the national average being about $800).
    - Annual cost of the state corporate renewal fee. (Varies state to state.)
    - May be subject to additional local or state occupational license fees or business assessments.

- The agent must become an employee of the corporation. Payroll requires additional paperwork and compliance requirements.
- Additional cost of consulting a CPA or knowledgeable advisor to insure the agent is aware of new responsibilities or compliance issues.

Reaping Rewards

When you start operating like a business owner—and not just an individual real estate agent who has hung her license with a local brokerage firm—you'll open yourself up to a number of benefits generally reserved only for legitimate businesses. They include, but are not limited to:

- Creating long-term, professional relationships with banks, accounting firms, financial planners, and others who can help you start and grow your entity.
- Establishing strong bonds with business groups, trade associations, and organizations, which in turn translate into more customers and referrals.
- Access to bank lines of credit, loans, and U.S. Small Business Administration-guaranteed loans.
- Recognition in the community and opportunities to raise your firm's profile by tapping sponsorship opportunities that range from little league teams to cultural events, and everything in between.
- An overall impression of professionalism and commitment to staying in business.

Because it can take time to start earning revenue as a real estate agent, one particularly good resource for agents just starting up or seeking growth funding is the SBA (www.sba.gov). Whether you're in need of startup capital or an infusion of cash to grow your existing company, this government entity is a logical "first step" on your road to getting financed. The organization doesn't make loans itself, but specializes in a host of loan guaranty programs that banks rely on when lending money to small companies.

Before you sit down with your banker, you'll need to get a handle on how much money you need, what it will be used for, and how it will be repaid. Existing businesses should also provide a history of when the company was started and how it has performed since inception as well as financial records such as a profit and loss statement for the last three years.

If your loan is approved, the bank funds it and the SBA guarantees a certain percentage based on the loan amount. If approved, the loan can be for working capital to buy inventory, furniture and fixtures, machinery and equipment, land for construction, building construction, leasehold improvements, and real property. From the small businesses whose loans it guarantees, the SBA is looking for repayment ability from the cash flow of the business, good character, management capability, collateral, and owner's equity contribution.

The SBA loan guarantees can be especially helpful for small business that can't come up with the collateral requirement that commercial lenders typically require. Most small businesses don't have a lot of collateral because they don't own their buildings, tend to be small in size, and have limited tangible assets that can be posted for collateral. This is an issue for a commercial lender working one-on-one with a small business, but lenders see things differently when the SBA guarantees the loan.

One of the first things any lender will consider during the loan process is credit history. Most lenders also use the following "five Cs of credit analysis," to determine your loan eligibility:

- **Capacity** to repay is the most critical of the five factors. The prospective lender will want to know exactly how you intend to repay the loan, and will consider the cash flow from the business, the timing of the repayment, and the probability of successful repayment of the loan.

- **Capital** is the money you personally have invested in the business and is an indication of how much you have at risk, should the business fail.

- **Collateral** is an additional form of security you can provide the lender. Giving a lender collateral means that you pledge an asset you own, such as your home, to the lender with the agreement that it will be the repayment source in case you can't repay the loan.

- **Conditions** focus on the intended purpose of the loan. Will the money be used for working capital, additional equipment, or inventory?

- **Character** is the general impression you make on the potential lender or investor. The lender will form a subjective opinion as to whether or not you are sufficiently trustworthy to repay the loan or generate a return on funds invested in your company.

Walk the Walk

In this chapter, we covered several business-related issues that real estate agents need to be aware of, and stressed the need for a "business ownership" mindset when working in the business. By thinking and operating like a business owner, you'll be more apt to break out from under your broker's wing and start promoting yourself and your services by taking active roles in REALTOR and related organizations, sponsoring events, and marketing yourself with a vengeance. Here are some other steps you can take to get yourself thinking like a business owner:

- Cut yourself a paycheck every week, biweekly or monthly, instead of just depositing your commission checks into your personal bank account.

- Get on a regular schedule of depositing estimated quarterly taxes.

- Create an "image" for your business that includes your photo, business logo, email, social handles, phone number, and a short

- tagline (such as, "Mr. Sold" or "Selling the Dream") to use on all correspondence, advertisements, and other materials.
- Investigate the possibility of incorporating, and research the various entities that are available to real estate agents in your state.
- Adopt the philosophy that it "takes money to make money," and don't be afraid to make affordable investments in technology, tools, office supplies, or other materials that will help you reach new customers and/or retain the ones you already have.
- Keep tabs on your business expenses and spend only what your business can cover without putting yourself in the red.
- Leverage technology, virtual assistants, outside resources, team members, and mentors to your advantage, even if you're working as a solo agent.
- Operate with the highest of ethical and legal standards at all times.

If you've spent a lot of time working in a salaried or hourly position, handling these and other business-related issues will be quite a change for you. Take heed because you're certainly not alone. Every year thousands of people make the pilgrimage from Corporate America to the real estate industry, to research new opportunities, more flexible work schedules, and a more gratifying career.

It's not always easy for them. One agent tells the story of how he struggled to learn how to sell himself, instead of selling a product, brand, or company. Coming from a 39-year career in Corporate America, where he worked in sales for a forest products manufacturer, the agent spent his first few months in real estate learning how to market himself as an individual agent.

"In Corporate America, I was well grounded. I knew exactly who I was and where I fit into the business and the industry," says the agent, who within four months had already sold one home and listed another.

"Taking the path of an independent agent has been a whole different world for me," says the agent, who has since come to realize that while real estate requires some teamwork, success really depends on how well agents can operate as business owners and truly differentiate themselves in a competitive marketplace.

As this agent learned, the key is to take it step by step, knowing that as each day passes it will become easier and easier to adopt the mindset of a business owner, rather than an employee. If you need more help getting your business on track, try one or more of these business resources:

- **Accounting and Financial Professionals:** A quick review of your financial statements by a trained eye can help detect slow collections, poor financial management, overextended accounts payables, or other warning signs early. Financial advisors can provide similar services, while accountants can be a big asset when it comes to issues like taxes and incorporating. Get referrals through the National Association of Personal Financial Advisors www.napfa.org and the American Institute of CPAs (AICPA), www.aicpa.org.

- **Financial Institutions:** Visit your bank for assistance with a line of credit, accounts receivable loan, or another vehicle to ease the cash crunch. Banks also provide ancillary services for their small business customers.

- **Business Groups:** Groups like your local chamber of commerce, the U.S. Small Business Administration (SBA), and the Service Corps of Retired Executives all offer programs and guidance for small business owners with financial questions. Business Networking International (BNI) and your local Chamber of Commerce both offer networking opportunities (among other services) for new business owners.

CHAPTER FIVE

Setting Goals and Objectives

Everyone has goals and objectives, no matter how trivial or undocumented those aspirations may sound to others. It could be as simple as getting a grocery order, or as complex as buying a home, but it's still an objective. Without them, everything would get done "on the fly" with no organization, and no way of knowing the benefits and rewards that came from attaining those objectives.

It works the same way in the business world: without objectives and goals, a business owner never really knows where she stands, what she's accomplished, and what she hopes to attain over short and long term. Know that there is a difference between goals and objectives:

- **Goals** are broad, long-range attributes that a business owner wants to accomplish. There are both primary goals (those that you want to achieve) and secondary goals (what you have to do or create to achieve these goals). They're not intended to be specific enough to act on, but simply state an overall ambition.

- **Objectives** are more specific targets of performance, and what we'll be discussing most in this chapter. Common business objectives include profitability, productivity, and growth. Because you basically are your own business as a real estate agent, your own objectives will also include personal and lifestyle-related issues.

A good way to get your goal and objective-setting exercise in gear will be to take a "big picture" look at your overall goals. You also want to think about how you'll achieve them and how you'll handle any goals that you do not achieve in the predetermined amount of time. Here's a goal assessment worksheet for you to use in order get these thoughts down:

1. What are my short-term goals? (For the next 6–12 months)

_____
_____
_____
_____

2. What are my long-term goals? (For the next 2–10 years)

_____
_____
_____
_____

3. Are my goals financially-based, satisfaction-based, or a combination of the two?

_____
_____
_____
_____

4. How will my business objectives affect my personal and life goals?

_____
_____
_____
_____

5. How realistic are these objectives?

_____
_____
_____
_____

6. How will I evaluate my success along the way?

_____
_____
_____
_____

7. What will I do if I don't achieve my goals?

_____
_____
_____
_____

If you worked through this exercise and are ready to dig a bit deeper to come up with more detailed objectives, then you're already miles ahead of the pack in your industry. According to one long-time management consultant, less than 5 percent of all real estate agents set goals. "Sure, they know how much they need to make in order to pay the bills, but they don't actually set goals so that they can strive for ever-greater rewards," says the consultant, who works often with agents, helping them to hone their business skills. "The fact is, we all know that the person who knows where they're going is sure to arrive."

Goal Setting 101

Right now, you're probably most interested in learning how to set realistic-yet-challenging objectives for your business, whether you've been working in it for one day or five years. The first step is to consider how satisfied you are with your current earnings. Then, factor in the time spent generating those earnings, and figure out if you can make the same amount of money in less time. Realize that money is not the only measure of success, and that the agent who works 75 hours a week for $350,000 in commissions annually, and the one who works 50 hours a week for $200,000, may both be meeting their objectives. A few good productivity podcasts to check out include Lead to Win, Extreme Productivity, and Getting Things Done.

"There are many different ways to look at your business. Not only in how much you are making, but in the amount of time it is taking and how much it is costing you to bring in that much revenue," says the consultant. "All of these issues come into play when you take the time to set goals."

Ask yourself these questions before setting objectives:

- Have I incorporated some time off into my schedule?
- Will I be able to take a vacation and recharge?
- Am I spending enough time with my family and friends?
- Am I taking enough time to myself, handling health-related issues and other important aspects of my life?

If you answered no to any of these questions, you'll want to tweak your objectives to include these important aspects of your life. The level of priority that you give them is a personal choice, but to avoid burnout, and health and family problems, be sure to factor your own needs and capabilities into the equation when setting objectives both for yourself, and for your business.

Laying it Out

Now it's time to get your objectives down on paper. We're going to take a look at the business-related points first, although later in this chapter you'll learn more about striking a workable balance in an industry where working weekends is the norm and customers know that you're armed with a cell phone (even outside of work hours).

For starters, make a list of everything you want to accomplish—both business and personal. Write down everything imaginable, then start paring it down. It's easy to get overwhelmed during this process because your list may be very long, but the key is to get yourself down to five solid objectives. "If you have too many, you'll lose focus and become discouraged," the consultant points out. "It's like going to a really great seminar where you hear many ideas that would be beneficial to your business. You come home and because there are so many you don't know which one to do first so consequently, you do nothing!"

When setting objectives, make sure you pick the kind that are:

- **Specific**, and as detailed as possible.
- **Measurable**, and able to be quantified.
- **Action-oriented**, and not dependent on certain "feelings" or "notions."
- **Realistic**, and attainable within the set amount of time.
- **Timely,** and completed within a certain timeframe.

When creating your own top objectives, you'll want to avoid lofty, generic objectives like:

- I want to sell more houses
- I want to find new customers
- I want to increase my income
- I want to use more technology to work more productively
- I want to do more business than the other agents in my office
- I want more time to myself, away from work

These types of statements will only drive you crazy. It's like saying that you "want to lose weight." It pays to be as specific as possible here, even if you have to break one "big" goal up into a number of smaller aspirations. Once your objectives are in place, write up a plan of action for achieving those objectives.

Here are a few good examples to follow:

Example #1: New Agents

- **Objective:** I want to increase the number of prospects that I reach on a weekly basis from five to 15 over the next three months.

- **Plan of action:** Expand my farm area by 250 homes and join two local organizations where I can network and schmooze with potential clients.

Example #2: Existing Agents Wanting to Grow

- **Objective:** I want to increase my annual earnings from $35,000 to $60,000 for the upcoming year.

- **Plan of action:** Working backwards, and basing the calculations on a 50/50 commission split with my broker on a gross commission rate of 6 percent, I'll need to close an additional $1 million in sales (four $250,000 homes) a year. Based on the assumption that one in 12 contacts turn into a sale, that means I'll have to make 60 additional contacts (or five per month) throughout the year.

Example #3: Existing Agents Looking to Scale Back

- **Objective:** By summer, I want to be able to increase the amount of quality time spent with my family and friends by 10 hours a week.

- **Plan of action:** I can either hire and train an assistant to handle my non-real estate activities (answering calls, creating digital content, mailing out postcards, etc.), hire a part-time licensed assistant to handle more of the real estate related tasks, or contract certain, day-to-day tasks to a virtual assistant on a per-project basis.

Pinpoint your objectives, write them down, make them quantifiable, and attach timeframes to them. Then refer back to them often to measure your progress and adjust your work and selling-style. "Many agents have told me that they have goals, but that they don't write them down," says one consultant. "When you write down your goals, your subconscious takes over and works on them as well."

Writing down your objectives provides another benefit: at the end of the year, when you take out that list that you worked on for the last 12 months, you'll know exactly what you did—and did not—accomplish. Expect it to either be a rewarding experience, a wakeup call, or somewhere in between.

When creating your business objectives, be sure to cover a range of areas within your business, including:

1. **Finance:** Improving profit, sales, or reducing costs or losses
2. **Customers:** Increasing customer satisfaction, choice, value
3. **Internal results:** Speeding up the delivery time to customers
4. **Growth and learning:** Increasing access to knowledge sources and developing organizational skills

Food for Thought

Setting objectives is particularly important for real estate agents, who are usually left to make or break themselves in an intense industry. While some companies will provide training that goes beyond just selling, you should go into it knowing that self-motivation and discipline will play a key role in your success. Through good planning, you'll be much better prepared to tackle challenges and overcome obstacles that are put in your way.

Use the following steps when setting up an overall business plan and tackling the objective-setting aspect of that plan:

- First, look at your closed transactions for the year before by property address. You want to know if it was from a buyer side, listing side, what the sales price was, and the amount of commission earned. From this you can determine your average sales price.

- Secondly, look at just your listings taken for the year before. Again, you want to note these by property address, date sold, or time taken off the market and the reason that a property didn't sell. You need to know what your percentage of listings sold to listings taken is.

- Next, look at your sources of business. Determine this by listings taken and also by buyer controlled sales. Note by property address what the source of the business was; e.g., farm, open house, for sale by owner (FSBO), referral, etc.

Now that you know where you have been, you can start laying out some important objectives. Here are some questions that will help you look at your business and pinpoint areas where you may need to set some solid objectives for the upcoming months:

- Did most of your sales come from the sale of your own listings?
- Did you get your listings from farming?
- Were your numbers of listings and buyer-controlled sales equal?
- Were there many referrals?
- Where did those referrals come from?
- Do your expenses correlate with where your business comes from?
- Are you spending the most in the area where you are getting the most business?
- Are you effectively using technology to work smarter, better, and faster?
- Is the marketplace the same climate as last year?
- What marketing activities can you beef up to help increase your revenue and deal with market changes?

When setting objectives, remember that business success is a very subjective term. What's good for one may not be good for another, so don't rely solely on other agents in your office to help shape your objectives. That's not to say you can't use the suggestions of wizened professionals to help you, it simply means that you should take that advice and use it to shape objectives that truly fit your own wants and needs.

Here are some other things to keep in mind as you set and conquer your objectives:

- **Be Flexible:** You don't want to change your goals and objectives every day, but realize that circumstances beyond your control may cause you to rethink your plan. Adjust it as you see fit, always making sure that your new objectives are in line with your longer-range planning strategies.

- **Break It Down:** If your plan is too long and hard to digest, break it down into several smaller, more manageable plans that you can sink your teeth into.

- **Ask Around:** Share your objectives with someone you trust and respect, and ask that person (or persons) to provide constructive feedback on the feasibility of these objectives.

- **Reward Yourself:** What good are goals if they don't come with rewards? Be sure to reward yourself (a weekend away once you close three sales in a 30-day period, for example) as significant milestones are accomplished.

- **Adjust Upwards:** You want your objectives to be attainable, but not too easy that they no longer motivate you to do better. If you're working through your objectives and reaching your goals in much shorter timeframes than predicted, you'll want to set the bar a little higher and give yourself something to work toward.

Staying Fresh

In real estate, goal setting helps you focus and succeed in an industry where burnout and frustration are common, and where a high number of new agents lose their drive and get out of the industry within 12 months of getting licensed.

By establishing goals, then setting objectives to help yourself reach those longer-term aspirations, you'll be one of the few agents who "stays fresh," even when business is tough. "Goals and objectives keep agents excited, and interested in the business," says one Texas broker. "We all need something to work toward, and to feel like we've truly accomplished something."

Having goals to work toward, and clear objectives to use as ladder rungs in achieving those aspirations, are key in the real estate industry, where the average agent closes 11 deals a year. That leaves a lot of downtime between commission checks—lapses that you can work through seamlessly with clearly defined objectives that are set in advance, adjusted accordingly, and used to measure longer-term success on a regular basis.

To set attainable and useful objectives, agents should first evaluate why they're in the real estate business in the first place. An agent who got her real estate license to earn a higher income, for example, would have different objectives than the one who signed up because a few family members found success in the business. "You really need to find the reasoning behind your desire to be in real estate, then use that information to drive your objectives and long-term goals," says the broker.

Agents who have been in the business for two or more years can take a slightly different approach by asking themselves where their customers are coming from and finding ways to better harvest those sources (and find new ones, of course). Here's an example:

> John hung his license at XYZ Realty two years ago, and has since seen his commission checks drop to undesirable levels. How can he set better objectives and work toward more effec-

tive long-term goals? Simple—he needs to look at where his business is coming from.

Let's say 20 percent of his business came from his own personal contacts or "sphere of influence," 20 percent from inbound and outbound phone calls, and 5 percent from the web. If John is spending 70 percent of his marketing budget on pay-per-click advertising, then he needs to rework his advertising approach to make better use of the sources that actually bring him business.

For John, that could mean setting an objective to join two new business groups within three months to help expand his sphere of influence, and hiring a part-time assistant to monitor his phone calls while he's on the road and unable to attend to that source of business.

One of the key areas where agents fall behind on their business objectives involves prospecting—or "getting out there" into their communities to find new customers. One real estate coach who works with both new and existing agents says the real culprit behind income fluctuations is not the industry's commission model, but rather the individual agent's ability to prospect and keep the pipeline filled with new business. Consistency counts, and can be cultivated by setting solid objectives on even a daily basis.

"To really understand where they're headed, agents should have a daily prospecting objective," says the coach, who urges agents to track over time the number of homes they're selling in relation to the volume of new prospects they're contacting. In other words, if you're turning one out of 10 contacts into customers, then you need to contact a proportionate number of prospects every day to meet your monthly sales goals.

And it's those sales goals that will help you measure your financial success in the industry, whether your goal is to become a multimillion dollar producer, or simply earn enough income to cover the bills and sock some away for retirement. As a real estate agent, you'll want to join this crowd of entrepreneurs and begin tracking your success right away. Doing so will help you not only outline a clear business path for your new career, but it will also help you:

- React objectively (rather than reactively in a "putting out fires" type of environment) to changing business climates, market conditions, and business challenges.
- Create a measure by which you can progress toward your objectives and goals.
- Keep on top of potential problems before they become detrimental to your company.
- Be less apt to make impulsive decisions that can hurt your business. (Such as firing an assistant when sales shrink, rather than figuring out where the dearth is and boosting a part of your business to stimulate financial growth.)

Making an Entrance

Every year, thousands of new real estate agents make their way into the industry. Between 2017 and 2018, in fact, the National Association of REALTORS® watched its membership increase by 80,000—a 6 percent increase that happened despite inventory shortages and rising home prices in many areas of the country.

In surveying its 1.3 million members, NAR announced that 29 percent have less than two years of experience. And, according to the Association of Real Estate License Law Officials (ARELLO), of the 2 million active real estate licensees in the U.S., the median tenure is four years.

In an industry where licensing courses don't teach agents how to actually conduct business, and where basic training simply doesn't cut it anymore (i.e., showing agents how to reach out to expired listings and then leaving them to their own devices), both new and existing licensees need more handholding than ever.

I recently interviewed a trainer and broker in Illinois who told me that her entrance into the industry was "100 percent the wrong way to do it," but says the certification work and other continuing education helped her make up the knowledge deficit fairly quickly. In fact, within just a few years in the business she'd sold $12 million in real estate and ranked in the top 10 percent of Chicago real estate agents.

"I learned the hard way that there's so much more to real estate than just getting a license; that's just entry-level," the agent says. "The question becomes, how are you going to build upon that foundation when it's just the starting line—not the end-all/be-all."

"There's a real disconnect in the market right now between wanting to make a killing in real estate because the market is great, and actually being trained on the fine points of how to sell real estate," another managing broker pointed out. "There's also a disconnect regarding who is supposed to be training whom and on what, and it should all start with the sponsoring brokerages and managing brokers; but that's not happening."

There are also business challenges to conquer. For example, new agents may hang their licenses with a broker, but that broker isn't necessarily his or her "employer." A highly entrepreneurial endeavor, real estate demands a level of persistence, diligence, and detail that many new agents haven't experienced in the past (and particularly if they moved over from the corporate world).

"New agents need business plans, they need to be able to follow the numbers, and they need research and data to do things right," says the first Illinois agent, who tells licensees to explore the business planning, market research, and data resources provided by both national and state REALTOR organizations.

Focusing Your Goals

Most real estate coaches and experts feel that agents don't do enough to set and achieve objectives during the course of business, and then the bulk of agents simply throw out general, unfocused goals (usually at the start of the New Year) without figuring out exactly what they need to do to get there. Here's a step-by-step process that you can start using right now to develop your own successful plan of attack:

1. **Be clear about exactly what you want:** Most agents either don't know what they want, want too much, or are unsure of why they want it. Others are worried about not achieving their goals and objectives, so they shy away from setting them. Remember that you have a 50 percent chance if you try, but a zero percent chance if you don't. Go for the 50/50 chance and see what turns up.

2. **Understand the objective- and goal-setting process:** We've heard the words "reach for your goals" our entire lives, but has anyone ever taught you exactly how to go about making that happen? Here are some guidelines you can start using right now in your own business:

   a. If failure weren't even possible, what would you want to accomplish over the next 12 months? As mentioned earlier in this chapter, stick to your five most important short-term goals. Be as specific as possible; make them measurable and set deadlines for each. Make each of them just out of reach, but not so far out of sight that they become too difficult to achieve.

   b. What will you gain by achieving these objectives? Look at both financial and personal gains and write down as many as you can think of.

   c. What will you miss out on by not achieving these objectives? This will be part of your motivation to succeed, so be honest with yourself.

   d. What could possibly prevent you from achieving these objectives? By recognizing the obstacles upfront, you'll be much better prepared to work through them if and when they're put in front of you.

   e. What resources or people can you tap to help achieve these objectives? Everyone from your broker to your family to the agents in your office can be facilitators during this process.

f. What actions or steps can you take right now to start working toward these objectives? Just because your overall business plan isn't complete yet, that doesn't mean you can't start turning your dreams into reality right now.

Getting Personal

Burnout runs rampant in the real estate industry, but that doesn't mean you have to fall prey to this common ailment. The good news is that you can avert burnout by integrating your own personal goals and objectives into your business plan. As an agent, you'll not only want to set financial goals for yourself and your firm, but you'll also want to dig a little deeper and establish some clear objectives for your own personal goals.

Whether you want to run in a marathon, start a family, or go on vacation for a week, it's vital that you keep these personal wants and needs in sight as you build your real estate business into a successful enterprise. It's sometimes easier said than done—particularly when a home closing is scheduled smack in the middle of your Caribbean vacation and can't be changed—but there are ways to get some balance into your hectic real estate career.

Why, you ask, is balance so critical when you're trying to write up a new business plan or develop better strategies for an existing practice? Because real estate agents are particularly prone to burnout and overwork, often through no fault of their own. "The public perception is that agents are accessible 24 hours a day, seven days a week," says one New Jersey-based agent who has been in real estate for 25 years. She bucks the 24/7 treadmill by working 40-hour workweeks and taking every Sunday off, without fail. She also removed her home number from the Multiple Listing Service (MLS) system, mostly as a way to keep other agents from disturbing her single day off.

"The biggest offenders are other agents," she says. "I used to get agents calling me on Sunday evening for feedback on a property that I showed a week prior. It was ridiculous." She also revels in activities that simply aren't cell-phone friendly—like skiing, and leaving the country and/or vacationing for at least four to six weeks out of the year. "Travel is one of my favorite hobbies," she adds, "and I've learned that it's very hard to get cell service in far-off countries (hint hint)."

This agent may know how to draw the line in the sand between work and play, but the typical agent does not. Concerned about missing "the big deal," upsetting a customer, or being left out of a major opportunity, many agents feel they simply must be available 24/7 or risk failure. "Most agents either live in survival mode, scared to miss any business," says Joeann Fossland, CEO at real estate coaching firm Advantage Solutions Group in Tucson, Ariz., "or they neglect to honor their own needs and say no to others, so they end up working 50–60 hours a week with no days off."

The technology movement has both helped and hindered the agent's ability to "get away." While agents no longer have to be tied to a desk to take phone calls—nor do they have to do as much driving around with clients (thanks to virtual tours)—today's agent spends more time monitoring email and connected to cell phones, tablets, and laptops.

For those agents who find themselves tethered to such devices seven days a week, the first degree of separation is taking off at least one 24-hour period every week. Schedule that time well in advance, says Fossland, and try not to let any "business" get in the way of your downtime. "Start communicating boundaries to everyone around you, set work hours and share them with your clients," adds Fossland, who also suggests including official "business hours" on your business cards, brochures, flyers, website, and email signatures.

Getting your family involved with your work goals can also be beneficial. "Let them know when you'll be available to them, and get them involved in goals—like a trip to Disneyland if you get 10 listings this month," she says. "It's a great way to turn the family into cheerleaders, instead of having them feel that you are ignoring them."

Agents concerned that a trip to Disneyland without the cell phone could translate into lost business will be surprised to find out that just the opposite is true. In fact, agents who consciously take downtime for themselves tend to be more productive, more enthusiastic, and healthier than their stressed-out counterparts. They're also choosier about what types of clients that they work with.

"Agents who are good at taking time off really don't miss anything," Fossland says. "That's because the agents who think they need 'everything that comes along' tend to work with high-maintenance clients rather than customers who respect their time, and who will wait until tomorrow to see a property."

Setting Yourself up for Success

Here is some sage advice on how to set yourself up for success, not burnout, as a residential real estate agent:

- Use the calendar on your mobile device and/or tablet to schedule your personal and family time, then work your real estate commitments in and around those important events.

- Take up a hobby, sport, or interest that allows you to "detach" from technology for at least a few hours out of the week.

- Accept the fact that you <u>do</u> need a vacation, and schedule one right now. This will give you a great goal to work towards as you build your business.

- If you're an overworked solo agent, consider hiring part-time or full-time help to handle mundane tasks that are keeping you from enjoying downtime.

- Explore the many different mobile applications and software solutions that help solo professionals get more productive <u>without</u> having to hire help.

- If you can't take a long vacation, schedule several "mini-breaks" throughout the year. Weekend getaways are a good way to unwind without being too far out of touch.

- Take Sundays (or any another 24-hour period) off every week to rejuvenate and recharge.

- On those days when you're "untouchable" (like on those Sundays when you're relaxing on your lanai with family and friends), don't check email, stay off Facebook and Twitter, and silence your cell. Enjoy time with your family, friends or solitude!

By establishing solid business objectives and goals and setting your sights on leading a balanced, fulfilling life, you'll be more apt to enjoy your position as a real estate agent, reach your short- and long-term goals, and attain the level of success that you've set forth for yourself.

New agents, in particular, should also understand the value of strategic planning. By creating a strategic plan for the future, setting goals, and working to achieve them, you'll not only be setting yourself up for success now, but you'll also be building a strong financial foundation for the next 10–20 years.

Be sure to involve your broker, accountant, financial planner, spouse, partner, or other important "voices" in the process, but don't be afraid to be your own guide throughout this process. And remember that there is no right or wrong way to do strategic planning; do what feels right and adjust accordingly as you go.

Borrowing a Page from a Top College

When the new crop of freshman students arrive at Dartmouth College every fall, the institution's Academic Skills Center knows that it has its hands full, trying to get freshly-minted high school graduates in "college" mode. To help, the center offers these tips that can apply across many different work and life situations:

1. Count all of your time as time to be used and make every attempt to get satisfaction out of every moment.
2. Find something to enjoy in whatever you do.
3. Try to be an optimist and seek out the good in your life.
4. Find ways to build on your successes.
5. Stop regretting your failures and start learning from your mistakes.

6. Remind yourself, "There is always enough time for the important things." If it is important, you should be able to make time to do it.
7. Continually look at ways of freeing up your time.
8. Examine your old habits and search for ways to change or eliminate them.
9. Try to use "waiting" time (such as when you are stuck in traffic, or in a doctor's waiting room) effectively.
10. Take notes on your smart phone or in a small notebook that you can carry around with you.
11. Examine and revise your lifetime goals on a monthly basis and be sure to include progress towards those goals on a daily basis.
12. Put up reminders in your home or office about your goals.
13. Always keep your long-term goals in mind.
14. Plan your day each morning or the night before and set priorities for yourself.
15. Maintain and develop a list of specific things to be done each day, set your priorities, and the get the most important ones done as soon in the day as you can. Evaluate your progress at the end of the day briefly.
16. Look ahead in your month and try and anticipate what is going to happen so you can better schedule your time.
17. Try rewarding yourself when you get things done as you had planned, especially the important ones.
18. Do first things first.
19. Have confidence in yourself and in your judgment of priorities and stick to them no matter what.
20. When you catch yourself procrastinating—ask yourself, "What am I avoiding?"
21. Start with the most difficult parts of projects, then either the worst is done or you may find you don't have to do all the other small tasks.

22. Catch yourself when you are involved in unproductive projects and stop as soon as you can.
23. Find time to concentrate on high-priority items or activities.
24. Focus on one thing at a time.
25. Put your efforts in areas that provide long-term benefits.
26. Push yourself and be persistent, especially when you know you are doing well.
27. Think on paper when possible; it makes it easier to review and revise.
28. Be sure and set deadlines for yourself whenever possible.
29. Delegate responsibilities whenever possible.
30. Ask for advice when needed.

CHAPTER SIX

Managing a Fluctuating Income

When you sign up for a sales career based solely on commissions, it doesn't take long to uncover the positives and negatives of the setup. On one hand, your paychecks are sizable, and unlimited in that there is no real "ceiling" prohibiting you from earning as much as you can. The checks can also come more frequently than the average paycheck, with some agents closing multiple deals per week based on the number of deals they do during a particular time period.

On the other hand, these checks are not always guaranteed, nor do they come at a predictable pace. The first quarter of the year you may take home $30,000 in commissions, for example, and the next quarter may be a bit leaner. These are the natural ebbs and flows of working on commissions, and they come with the territory. (If it's any consolidation, most small business owners have to manage the same financial fluctuations.)

If you're used to taking home a weekly or biweekly paycheck, the first year or so of managing those fluctuations can be difficult. Through good budgeting, an effective marketing strategy (to keep the client "pipeline" full), and an honest look at your own financial house, you'll find yourself much better prepared to handle the fluctuations that are sure to come your way.

The Basics

Just how much can you expect to earn as a real estate agent depends on a few critical factors:

- **How much time you put into the business:** Part-timers will generally not make as much as those working the business 40 to 60-plus hours per week.

- **The size of your own networking circle:** Those agents who have a steady flow of potential buyers and sellers at their fingertips tend to do more deals that those who start from scratch on each new deal.

- **Your effective use of technology and related tools:** The agent who totes around a laptop with real-time access to the local Multiple List System (MLS), for example, can print out Comparative Market Analyses (CMA) for a potential seller in a flash (compared to the agent who has to go back to the office to do it, then deliver it or fax it to the customers), then use the time saved to sell more.

- **Your broker's training program:** Brokers that offer regular training and who work closely with their agents tend to cultivate more successful salespeople.

- **Your broker's compensation arrangement:** It ranges from a 50/50 split (of gross commissions) to a 100 percent arrangement, and everything in between. Keep in mind that those brokers that take higher cuts tend to offer more advertising and marketing support, training and related necessities than the 100 percent companies. In 2017, 35 percent of agents were compensated under a fixed commission split (under 100 percent), according to NAR, 25 percent with a graduated commission split (increases with productivity), and 14 percent with a capped commission split (rises to 100 percent after a predetermined threshold).

- **Your commitment to the business:** If you got into real estate to make a quick buck, you'll probably be disappointed. Most of the agents who are earning high annual salaries have thoroughly committed to the business. They're in it for the long haul, and realize that it can take years to build a small business into a profitable entity.

Several different organizations track real estate agents' earnings (see Chapter 2 for all of NAR's salary numbers and related statistics), so let's take a look at the numbers that the U.S. Bureau of Labor Statistics puts out. These numbers are usually considered low by industry standards, but they will give you a good idea of the various earnings levels of the nation's residential agents.

According to the BLS, the median annual earnings of salaried real estate agents, including commissions, were $47,880 or $23.02 per hour in 2017 (the most recent numbers available at press time). For real estate brokers—who have additional education, testing and experience requirements—that figure increases to about $57,000. Overall, the highest 10 percent of agents earned more than $109,490 in 2017.

In real estate, income usually increases as an agent gains experience, but individual ability, economic conditions, and the type and location of the property also affect earnings. When you're in sales and you are active in community organizations and in local real estate associations, you can broaden your sphere of influence and increase your earnings, according to the BLS, which reports that a beginning agent's earnings often are irregular, because a few weeks or even months may go by without a sale.

Like many other commission jobs, real estate sales is an arena where some brokers will allow an agent to draw against future earnings from a special account (note that the practice is not "typical" for new employees). The new agent, therefore, should have enough money to live for about six months, or until commissions increase. This can be a moving target for some new agents, so it's generally advisable to have a six to 12-month reserve on hand before getting into the business. If you begin collecting checks before that reserve runs out, all the better. If you don't, at least you know you're covered and able to concentrate on building your business—not wondering how you're going to pay your bills—during that first year in business.

Hurdling Challenges

Ask any real estate expert what the average agent's biggest challenge is, and the answer will probably be "sustaining himself from the time he closes the sale until he gets paid." For the average sale, that can take 60 to 90 days, although it varies from deal to deal. In a brisk seller's market, for example, all-cash deals can close in an as few as 15 to 30 days. After helping with the negotiations and purchase agreement, the listing and/or selling agent will perform these and other important tasks:

- Coordinating inspections and other events
- Fielding calls and answering questions from buyer or seller (depending on which one the agent is representing)
- Keeping tabs on the mortgage lending process to be sure it's on track
- Documenting all activities related to the sale
- Managing the necessary disclosures and related paperwork
- Arrange for mold, asbestos, roof or other inspections
- Coordinating with escrow to be sure it is opened in a timely fashion
- Verifying with the escrow holder that the deposit was placed in escrow and that funds are sufficient
- Reviewing escrow documents with seller
- Making arrangements to have all utilities on and operating during the entire escrow period (if property is vacant)
- Making arrangements to meet buyer and/or the cooperating agent at all requested inspections

- Reviewing and discussing with seller any requested repairs by buyer
- Meeting with the appraiser
- Coordinating any other items that need to be completed prior to close of escrow
- Reviewing closing statements with seller and/or buyer
- Making arrangements for buyer to receive keys to the property
- Ensuring that all parties know the closing dates, times, and location

As you work your way down this list, keep your eye on the prize: that commission check that comes your way on closing day. For agents, all roads lead to that short period of time at the title company or attorney's office when the loan documents are signed and checks are distributed for those service providers who worked on the deal, including you. To avoid living "commission check-to-commission check," you'll want to make sure your own client pipeline is filled enough to keep those checks coming in at a regular pace. This also ensures that closing delays on certain deals don't impact your finances too severely, as such delays are fairly common in the real estate industry.

The Highs and Lows

There are other ways to ride out the highs and lows of commission life, and they circle back to the earlier chapter on treating your business like a business. A line of credit from a local bank, for example, can help even out the fluctuations by providing a financial cushion when times are lean.

When applying for business loans and/or lines of credit, you'll probably be asked to personally guarantee the repayment (particularly if you're new to the business), and the total amount will be based on a percentage of your company's annual sales. Let's say you expect $60,000 in revenues for the upcoming year, then the bank may be willing to lend you $5,000 to $10,000 on a line of credit to use as needed. Check with banks in your area for specific details on what programs they offer.

Develop a Budget

Budgeting is also critical for real estate agents, as is investing for the future (see Chapter Nine, Long-Term Financial Planning) and being able to meet your own financial obligations while you help clients either sell their homes, or purchase new dwellings. Don't neglect your own needs during the process. Be sure to pay yourself an adequate compensation (from your month's commission checks) that covers not only those financial obligations, but also provides adequate money to "live on" for the month. Here's how to make that happen, no matter what stage of the game you're at:

- **Brand new agent:** Expect to live off your own personal savings, line of credit, or other resource for the first six months. If a sale comes sooner, all the better. When that first check does come in, use this formula to create a healthy balance between your own needs and those of your business. Let's say it was a $3,750 commission check (based on the sale of a $250,000 home, split with the cooperating broker and split 50/50 with your own broker).
  - First, deposit $2,000 to your personal bank account, for living and personal expenses and savings
  - Then, set aside 25 percent for taxes, or $937.50 (adjust according to your tax bracket)
  - Lastly, reserve the remaining $1,000 to either pay off business expenses you've incurred during the last month, or retain that money for future business use
- **Existing agent:** Commission checks aren't new to you, but for some reason you just can't seem to manage the fluctuations associated with your commission-only sales job. If this describes

you, try taking that next $5,000 commission check and dividing it up like this:

- $2,500 to pay your own bills and expenses, and cover your lifestyle needs
- $1,250 to set aside for taxes (based on a 25 percent tax bracket)
- $1,000 to pay off business expenses incurred in the last month, such as MLS or REALTOR association dues
- $250 reserved in a business account for future use, such as setting up a retirement account

These formulas are not set in stone, and are based on the assumption that you know exactly how much money you need each month not only to live comfortably, but also to run your business. If you don't have a handle on this aspect of your career yet, please refer to Chapter Two, Business Planning 101, for an in-depth look at the components that make up your monthly budget and how to adequately cover them, even if you're just starting out in the business. Using a program like Quickbooks or an online accounting platform like Freshbooks to track your monthly income and expenditures (both personal and professional), will give you yet another tool that you can use to manage a fluctuating income.

Filling Your Business Pipeline

As a real estate agent, you'll make money by meeting people and turning them into home buyers and sellers. This is an oversimplification, of course, but I'm saying is that YOU are your best tool for managing a fluctuating income. The more people you get out there and meet, the more past connections you reconnect with, and the more online leads you follow up on, the richer your business pipeline will be.

And with a full client pipeline, the odds are good that your checks will be more frequent and predictable. So, while fluctuations are typical from time to time, it doesn't necessarily mean that you're going to spend the next 20 years of your life wondering where your next paycheck is going to come from.

One Texas broker says the key to keeping the pipeline full is to plan for the long-term, instead of just working on one paycheck at a time. Just like a small business owner wouldn't serve one client from start to finish—then go in search of another—the agent shouldn't put all of his time and energy into closing one deal before moving on to the next one. Look beyond today, and realize that in order to keep your income as steady as possible, you'll need access to a regular supply of:

- Potential buyers who are looking to purchase new homes now

- Potential buyers who may be ready to buy within the next three to 12 months

- Homeowners who are ready to sell their homes now

- Homeowners who are ready to sell within the next three to 12 months

If all four of these categories are covered (some clients may not "fit" perfectly, such as the buyer who is ready to purchase in 60 days, but this gives you a general idea), you'll be assured a steady flow of business possibilities.

How you divide up your daily activities is equally as important, since the social nature of the real estate profession has a way of bogging you down with tasks that don't generate commission checks. Floor time, during which you man the office phones for potential clients, can be very productive, for example. These days, much of those client interactions actually take place online—with you being the "agent of the day" or holding some other title that puts you in direct contact with the leads generated online. Time spent standing by the coffee pot waiting for that phone to ring, however, can be better spent on marketing and advertising activities, calling friends and family to remind them that you're there to help if they want to buy or sell, or updating your website to reflect updated listings and information.

At the Texas brokerage, for example, both new and existing agents are advised to divide their time between current clients (in the interest of generating referral business from them), handling their active listings and/or pending contracts, and generating new business by reaching out to prospective buyers and sellers. "Divide your day or week into three equal parts, and be sure to put adequate time into these three different activities," says the broker. "The agents that do this find that they get their incomes on a more even keel."

Taking the "thirds" approach ensures that you're not only working the business that's in front of you at the moment, but that you're also cultivating existing relationships and building new ones all the time. Doing so virtually ensures that you'll not only be lining up commission checks for the next few months, but that you'll also be setting yourself up for longer-term success, since all of your clients will not be ready to buy or sell at the same time. That person you met at the Rotary meeting last week who mentioned that she is moving out of state in six months, for example, is actually a very warm lead who in six months' time could turn into a "hot" prospect.

"Too many agents stop prospecting while in the middle of a transaction, and are then forced to start all over again 30 to 60 days later when the deal closes," says the broker. "This is not a good approach, and it's what leads to major income fluctuations that can eventually lead to failure. On the other hand, those agents who focus on all three aspects of their business gain stability, and avoid the stress of having to deal with the ups and downs of working on commission."

Yet another way to keep such stressors at bay is by saving some money in reserve for the lean times. This isn't always easy for newer agents, but there's really no excuse for those entrenched agents to not sock away some money from each check for a rainy day. If you need to open a separate account, deposit $1,000 from each check into it, go for it. Money market accounts—which pay slightly higher interest rates than regular savings accounts—are a good option. Whatever investment vehicle you choose, the key is to create a cushion on which to fall back on should you ever need to go more than two to four weeks without a commission check.

Prospect, Prospect, Prospect

A real estate agent's income will fluctuate in direct proportion to how well she prospects, plain and simple. That means if an agent slacks off on finding new customers, generating referrals, or cultivating her existing customer base, she'll definitely feel it in the wallet. "Agents need to have consistency about their work habits," says the real estate coach. "They can't back off just because they've had a few sales, nor should they go into panic mode if they haven't made a few sales."

To strike that balance between "making enough" sales and not entering panic mode, schedule regular customer-generation activities that include (but that aren't limited to):

- Farming, or selecting a specific neighborhood, community, or "farm area" to market yourself and your services to on a regular basis. Stick flags in their yards on the Fourth of July, drop off seed packets during planting season, or just knock on doors and introduce yourself.
- Direct mail pieces (Just Sold, Just Listed, etc.)
- Web ads (banners, a website, Google AdWords, etc.)
- Facebook, Twitter, and Instagram
- QR codes on your yard signs and flyers
- Online lead generation systems like Realtor.com, Zillow, or BoldLeads
- Advertising in online and print publications
- "Warm" calling potential customers with whom you've had prior contact
- Calling For Sale By Owner (FSBO) listings
- Contacting "expired" or "cancelled" listings from the local MLS

- Reaching out to anyone else in your own network who may be ready to buy or sell in the next one to 12 months

- Asking past clients for two to three of their friends, family, or colleagues who may need an agent now, or in the near future

You'll probably come up with more creative ways to find customers as your career progresses, but no matter the method, the key is to keep doing it on a daily basis even if you feel that you're "busy enough." As with any business, it's the marketing and advertising activities that get shelved first when business is good.

To keep the momentum going in your own business, and avoid future panic attacks, be sure to stay current on your prospecting at all times. This alone will play a key role in just how many ups and downs your income will experience throughout a year's time.

Cracking the Online Lead Code

Converting online "visitors" into legitimate buyers and sellers has become a full-time job for today's agents.

"In real estate, the goal is always to get your listings or information out to as many as people as possible, and the web is a great place to do that," says one broker-owner. "Instead of just putting the listing in the MLS and a sign in the yard, we're now able to leverage a lot of different networks, including social media."

But with the increased exposure and number of "hits," comes the responsibility of following up with those potentials with the goal of at some point transforming them into paying customers. "Online lead generation is definitely a numbers game," he continues. "Or more specifically, it's a giant funnel that you really have to sift through to get to the legitimate, interested customers."

The good news is that many agents are bucking low online conversion rates by utilizing existing lead-generation platforms in interesting ways and/or recording sales that originated online but that can't always be traced back to a single interaction or platform. Here are three ways that they're cracking the code:

Hit "Boost" on Facebook: The online social media platform is a hotbed for everything real estate-related, and that makes it a great lead-generation tool for agents. Facebook is a good platform because you can get in and generate leads relatively cheaply, says the broker-owner, whose last campaign cost about 80 cents per lead. To maximize that investment, hit the Facebook "boost this post" button for listings. You can select recipients to push the post—which is initially published on a Facebook business page—out to a larger audience.

Build a great database: Facebook itself is great, but unless you have a platform for collecting leads, you're not going to get the most out of the platform," says one broker/trainer. And once the mechanisms are in place to collect the leads—be it a corporate website, a landing page, or some other platform—he says agents can make them more powerful by simply giving something away (i.e., "Sign up today for a weekly update on real estate activity in your area" or "Email me for a list of the top 10 home staging tips"). Give away something of value without an ask, says the broker-owner, who has had particularly good success with a "day in the life" online video that breaks down a specific aspect of the real estate market or sales process into easy-to-view clips.

Get ready to respond quickly: Facebook's auto-reply feature is another tool that allows you to instantly reply to any message even if you're too busy to write a personal note at the time. Whether someone is using Facebook, Instagram, Twitter or any other online lead generation tool, the trick is to have your phone in hand like a gun in a holster, one agent says. "You have to be ready to respond at all times, even if you can't or if you don't really want to."

Here are seven more tips to making the most out of your online leads:

1. Use the lead-generation platform's built-in tools to get more out of your listings. On Facebook, for example, the boost and auto-responder functions can help you reach more people with little extra effort.

2. Don't confuse information requests with online leads. Every agent has converted a lead from a basic offer to do a home valuation, but that doesn't necessarily translate into a closed deal.

3. Finish what you started. If you start a Twitter profile, finish it. If you start using Instagram, follow through with it. Polish everything on a regular basis and make sure you're being complete, thorough, and consistent.

4. Review your timeline regularly. Delete stuff that you really don't want on there permanently and create a professional presence that allows people to really "dig into" who you are.

5. Keep up with your offline lead generation efforts. If you're working a certain zip code, neighborhood, or subdivision, then you should also be doing mailings in those areas, with an emphasis on your just-listed, under-contract, and just-sold listings. This will go a long way in reinforcing your online lead generation efforts.

6. Develop a follow-up process. Knowing that the next agent is just a mouse click or two away, be sure to use a combination of personal notes and auto-responders to let prospects know that you're a "real" person who is handling their request.

7. Be the expert. If you get someone on the phone who's asking about a house in a subdivision or particular price point, make sure you have that information down pat. "Quietly dazzle them with information," one real estate trainer suggests.

Tracking Your Progress

Once you've established a prospecting plan, you'll want to keep close track of just how well those activities are paying off for your business. For example:

- If you're a **new agent** and you've spent two hours on the phone each day contacting FSBOs and expired listings, but haven't gotten a listing of your own in the last 90 days, then it's pretty clear it's time to tweak your prospecting activities to include more productive strategies. You may, for example, want to instead select a specific "farm" area of about 200 homes and begin sending direct mail to them, highlighting your expertise in that area and willingness to provide homeowners with a free Comparative Market Analysis (CMA) during the next 30 days.

- If you're an **existing agent** in search of better results from your prospecting, create a chart (on an Excel or Google Drive spreadsheet) that categorizes your activities, how much time spent on each, and number of sales or listings that have come as a result of that prospecting. If a certain area isn't producing results (say, calling potential customers with whom you already have a non-business relationship) it's probably time to spend less time on it and instead invest in an online lead generation membership or expand your network by joining a local business group.

Market Knowledge

Just how well you know your own market can play a role in your financial success as an agent. Through basic market research and knowledge, you can dig pretty deeply into your market's statistics to figure out how many homes are sold annually—compared to the total number of homes—and estimate what percentage of that market you'll be able to tap as a residential agent. "I'm often shocked at how naïve agents are about this," says one real estate coach. "They don't even look at the basic turnover rates."

Nationally, for example, there are more than 135 million single-family homes and condominiums. In 2017, about 614,000 homes were sold in the U.S. and the current homeownership rate is about 64 percent, according to Statista's U.S. Residential Housing—Statistics & Facts. In its 2018 Profile of Home Buyers and Sellers, NAR says that:

- Buyers of new homes made up 14 percent and buyers of previously owned homes made up 86 percent.
- Most recent buyers who purchased new homes were looking to avoid renovations and problems with plumbing or electricity at 38 percent. Buyers who purchased previously-owned homes were most often considering a better price at 32 percent.
- Detached single-family homes continued to be the most common home type for recent buyers at 82 percent, followed by eight percent of buyers choosing townhomes or row houses.
- Senior-related housing stayed the same this year at 13 percent, with 18 percent of buyers typically purchasing condos and 11 percent purchasing a townhouse or row house.
- There was a median of only 15 miles between the homes that recent buyers purchased and the homes that they moved from.
- Home prices increased slightly in 2018 to a median of $250,000 among all buyers. Buyers typically purchased their homes for 99 percent of the asking price.
- The typical home that was recently purchased was 1,900 square feet, had three bedrooms and two bathrooms, and was built in 1991.

NAR also says that the most frequently purchased housing type among all buyers was a detached single-family home. Single females and single males were the most likely to have purchased a townhouse or row house, over any other household type. The share of senior-related housing purchases was 13 percent in 2018, holding steady from the previous year.

Overall, buyers expect to live in their homes for 15 years, according to NAR's report. The expected tenure increased with age, and was also higher among repeat buyers. The biggest factor that would cause a buyer to move from their newly purchased home was due to life changes, including additions to their family, marriage, children moving out, or retirement. While 27 percent of buyers reported that life changes could cause them to move, NAR reports that 19 percent of recent buyers said that this was their "forever home" and had no intention of moving.

Similar information is available at the local level from either your REALTOR association or MLS, and can be invaluable when trying to figure out how to best spend your valuable prospecting time. Here's an example that both new and existing agents can use:

- **Size of the farm area:** 1,000 homes (fill in the number of homes in your targeted farm area)

- **Turnover rate:** 5.0 percent (adjust this percentage to coincide with the appropriate percentage for your own region)

- **Number of homes that will sell in that specific area every year:** 50 homes

In this example, the agent with the powerful marketing program will probably capture about 50 percent of that market, resulting in 25 sales annually. This is a good frame of reference for any agent, particularly the one who wants to close 100 transactions annually and realizes that to do this, she must quadruple the size of her farm area. "Most agents aren't thinking about this," says the coach. "I know agents who have a farm area of 150 homes with a turnover of 3 percent, or five homes a year. That person would need 100 percent market share to even have a chance of surviving as an agent."

Be sure to factor in market conditions when selecting farm areas, since real estate's cyclical nature can distort that turnover rate from year to year. If the area is too small by the standards outlined above, for example, a slightly depressed real estate market for 12 to 24 months will certainly wreak havoc on your income. Competition is another important consideration, since going head-to-head with an agent who has dominated a particular farm area for years could produce depressing results.

"You really don't want to take on a dominant agent in his or her own marketplace," the real estate coach points out. "Too often, new and growing agents will target an area where another agent is experiencing great success, without doing the market research to find out what chance they have of really penetrating that market."

If you're an existing agent whose sales are growing at 5 to 10 percent (or higher) annually, you'll want to step back and look at the key issues mentioned above, such as:

- Putting time every day into prospecting for new buyers and sellers

- Thoroughly examining your market, including home turnover statistics

- Using those statistics to determine if your current farm area is adequate, or if it needs to be expanded or replaced

- Checking out the competition in your marketplace, particularly in your farm area

- Ask yourself: is there something else that might be eroding my client base?

"If you're stagnating, then you definitely need to tweak your plan," says the real estate coach. "There should be a steady, upward trend in an agent's real estate sales based on natural client-generation tools, such as referrals." And while referrals are a great source of business, they shouldn't be your only revenue stream. To pump up sales, achieve your financial goals and avoid income fluctuations, you must also feed your client pipeline with new marketing efforts.

Get Organized

If there's one missing link that CPAs tend to notice about most real estate agents, it's the need for better organization. A real estate licensee himself, one California CPA says agents usually lack a separate business account, for example, and are remiss when it comes to documenting business expenses.

"One of the first steps an agent should take in getting their finances on track is to open a business bank account, and not operate out of their personal account," says the CPA. "If they ever were to be audited, this separates their personal activity and helps to avoid exposing that activity to unwanted review." It also assists persons who are just starting out in a business to establish the bona fide nature of their activities. This can be important when a startup net operating loss is encountered.

Using a dedicated business credit card is another good way to separate business from personal, as are the various loans or lines of credit available to today's business owners. The CPA also suggests a home equity line of credit, which can help even out the fluctuations associated with working in a cyclical, commission-based business. Since earnings will change from year to year, good tax planning is equally as essential (See Chapter Seven, Tax Planning, for more information) as are investment vehicles like college savings accounts, retirement plans, and insurance policies.

Knowing that these important financial components are in place—and that they're funded by your income—can help you stay on track with both the prospecting and selling side of the real estate business. While a part-time agent may be able to afford to slack off once in a while to focus on other things, for example, the full-time agent whose retirement accounts and college savings funds are waiting for cash infusions will be more apt to strive for a steady, predictable income.

"You need to be able to normalize your expected income over an entire year, keep track of your earnings, and know exactly where you stand financially at any given time," the CPA says. By tracking income on a quarterly and annual basis, for example, you'll be better equipped to make accurate, estimated tax payments that avoid penalties when April 15th rolls around.

Whether you maintain those records on an Excel spreadsheet or with online or offline financial software (Quickbooks, Freshbooks, etc.), the key is to create an organized, easy-to-access and updated method, and you'll soon find yourself much better equipped to deal with any income fluctuations thrown your way.

CHAPTER SEVEN

Tax Planning & Preparation

Although they may hang their licenses on a broker's wall and work in the office on a regular basis, agents truly are the masters of their own domains when it comes to taking care of their tax obligations, tracking expenditures and income, and filing in a timely, accurate manner according to predetermined schedules.

One agent found this out quickly after leaving her IT job a few years back in search of greener pastures. She found these pastures in residential real estate, a field where she could control her own destiny and have more flexibility. It didn't take long for this now-successful, Florida-based agent to find out just how much she'd taken on by leaving her paycheck behind, particularly on the tax management front.

"The first year or so, I really did no business or tax planning," says the agent, who works with another REALTOR in a partnership arrangement. "The transition from salaried information technology manager to small business owner wasn't easy." While the pair knew they had to put away 25–30 cents of every dollar earned to cover tax liabilities, she says they still lacked basic tax planning knowledge. As a result, deadlines came as a surprise, as did total tax amounts due for estimated taxes and self-employment tax (which takes 15.3 percent off a sole proprietor's income).

"We really didn't have control of the situation," the agent says. "It kind of hit us by surprise because we always knew we had to plan, but actually sitting down and planning out a year in advance and putting it on paper was a different story. During the first year or so, everything just kind of hit us after the fact."

After "winging it" for those first 12–18 months and getting hit with tax liabilities and penalties for not making adequate estimated payments, the agent used her experience in the technology field to develop a number of Microsoft Excel spreadsheets to use for budgeting and business planning.

Both she and her partner then incorporated their companies as Subchapter S corporations, and completely separated their personal finances from their business finances. The final piece of the puzzle was Quicken for personal finances and QuickBooks to manage monthly, quarterly and yearly income and expenses.

"Once we started planning during that second year, it all kind of fell into place," the agent recalls. "We realized that we had to have completely separate business and personal financial plans, and that planning really pays off when it comes to taxes."

Taxing Matters

Faced with a full workload, demanding clients, the need to make a living, and only so many hours in the day to do so, real estate agents tend to get caught off guard when tax time rolls around. Because commission checks are paid in full, with no taxes withheld, agents are largely on their own when it comes to managing their taxes. Poor recordkeeping is usually the biggest culprit. Busy tracking down listings, spending time with clients, and handling other activities that bring in the money, agents tend to ignore issues like creating potential tax deductions, gathering and recording receipts, budgeting, and tax planning.

In fact, most CPAs who have spent time working with agents will tell you that few agents properly plan their finances, and as a result wind up grappling with the tax system. At the heart of the problem are those agents who don't think of themselves as business owners, and as such don't organize business receipts, keep separate business records, form corporations, and/or maintain separate checking accounts.

Tax Planning & Preparation

"At the end of the year most agents are disorganized, scrambling around to find receipts and records," says one CPA who works often with agents, and who advises them to completely separate their real estate activities from their personal finances. That means opening a separate checking account and credit card account, and using them only for depositing commission checks and paying out expenses like advertising, overhead, and travel. That way, when April 15th or October 15th rolls around (depending on whether you filed an extension this year or not and if your business is incorporated), you won't have to pore over bank and credit card statements to separate personal from business expenses and income.

You'll also want to get a handle on exactly what is expected of you, tax-wise, or risk falling behind and incurring stiff penalties for non-compliance. As a self-employed individual, you may be responsible for completing the following forms. Check with your individual city and state for income and related tax requirements, and follow these IRS filing guidelines for self-employed individuals:

- If you are self-employed, a sole proprietor (someone who owns an unincorporated business by yourself), or an independent contractor, you are required to report income and expenses on **Schedule C or C-EZ** and calculate your earnings that are subject to self-employment tax (which is 15.3 percent). Attach the schedule to your Form 1040, U.S. Individual Income Tax Return.

- If you are a member of a partnership that carries on a trade or business, your distributive share of its income or loss from the trade or business is included in your net earnings from self-employment. The partnership must report the business income and expenses on **Form 1065**, U.S. Return of Partnership Income, along with a Schedule K-1 showing each partner's net income, and file Schedule SE (Form 1040) to report your individual SE tax.

- If you have employees, you must pay **employment taxes**, including Federal Income, Social Security, and Medicare taxes.

- **Estimated tax** is the method used to pay (including SE tax) on income not subject to withholding. You generally have to make estimated tax payments if you expect to owe taxes, including self-employment tax, of $1,000 or more when you file your return. Use Form 1040-ES to figure and pay the tax. You must make estimated tax payments and file Form 1040-ES if both of these apply:
  - Your estimated tax due is $1,000 or more.
  - The total amount of your tax withholding and refundable credits is less than the smaller of:
    - 90 percent of the current tax year's tax liability
    - 100 percent of the last tax year's liability

Creating a Streamlined System

One of the best ways to deal with tax issues is to establish a budget for the entire year, then use those figures to estimate tax liabilities, which are due every quarter year-round. You'll also want to find an accounting system that suits your own work style, which these days typically means using financial software or an online platform like Freshbooks, NetSuite, Sage One, or Quickbooks Online. Enter any expenses incurred (gas, meals, advertising expenses, etc.) in the program and then retain the actual receipt in a regular file.

Realize that certain business expenses may be tax deductible, such as supplies, advertising fees, travel expenses, and your home office, to a certain percentage. Writing off legitimate expenses is important in reducing your tax liability, but be sure to only take the right percentage of legitimate deductions (consult with your tax advisor on this point). Keep receipts/proof of any and all deductions you plan to take, and be sure that the costs are indeed business expenses. To be deductible, a business expense must be both ordinary (common and accepted in

Tax Planning & Preparation

your field of business) and necessary (helpful and appropriate for your business).

A few of the most common business deductions are:

- Bad debts
- Car and truck expenses
- Depreciation
- Employee pay
- Insurance
- Interest
- Legal and professional fees
- Rent
- Pension plans
- Taxes (federal, state, local and foreign)
- Travel, meals and entertainment
- Business use of your home
- Advertising
- Education expenses
- Licenses and regulatory fees
- Subscriptions to trade or professional journals
- Utilities

Here are a few more Realtor-specific expenses that you may be able to claim on your tax return:

- Continuing Education
- Desk Fees
- Client Gifts
- Conventions and Conferences Signage
- Marketing and Advertising Costs
- Real Estate Software and Applications

- MLS Dues
- Professional Dues

Within each of these deduction categories there are sub-categories and rules that spell out whether particular deductions are indeed legitimate or not. Since you probably don't have time to look up the validity of every business expense for deduction purposes, the best measure is to develop a process of organizing the receipts on a daily or weekly basis, year-round.

"Never wait until April to plow through the drawer full of unrecognizable receipts," cautions one Florida-based CPA. "Unless it is an asset like office equipment or furniture, the IRS usually does not care <u>when</u> you paid for an expense during the year, so categorize receipts by type of expense."

If you don't already have a system in place for this, try the very simple brown envelope system. At the start of each year, pull out a dozen 9-inch by 12-inch brown mailing envelopes and label them by type of expense, such as:

- Advertising/marketing expenses
- Automobile expenses (Be sure to also keep a written or digital mileage log detailing your business miles.)
- Books, newspapers, periodicals and subscriptions
- Dues and fees: MLS, local REALTOR board, etc.
- Gifts (note: this is limited to $25 per person or related couple)
- Meals & Entertainment (note: this type of expense is only 50 percent deductible)
- Miscellaneous (use only when needed, and always notate a detailed description)
- Office supplies
- Postage
- Refreshments (100 percent deductible)
- Seminars/education

- Technology-related expenses
- Telephone
- Tolls & parking fees
- Travel

At the end of each day, empty your pockets or purse and sort receipts into the appropriate envelope. Be sure to always write the amount on the front of the envelope, so that at the end of the year, there's no need to paw through unreadable papers. "Just total the numbers on the front of the envelope and Voila!" says the CPA. "And, the best part is that the expenses are already categorized."

Estimated Tax Payments

If you're accustomed to a regular paycheck and weekly deductions from your gross income, then making estimated tax payments will be by far one of the biggest adjustments you'll make as a real estate agent. One successful real estate agent in Illinois prefers to use customized Excel spreadsheets for tax planning and tracking. He developed them himself, and uses them to:

- Track expenses and plan a yearly budget, based on sales projections.
- Adjust the budget when necessary.
- Utilize the data to file yearly tax returns and estimate quarterly tax payments.
- Base those estimated payments either on 90 percent of the current year's income expectations, 100 percent of last year's income, or 110 percent of last year (use the latter if you made over $150,000). This is known as the IRS' "safe harbor" estimated tax payment.

- Adjust estimated tax payments higher or lower, depending on annual sales level (to risk getting hit with a penalty for underpayment).

To figure your own estimated tax, you must factor in your expected adjusted gross income, taxable income, taxes, deductions, and credits for the year. It may be helpful to use your income, deductions, and credits for the prior year as a starting point. Refer to your federal tax return as a guide, and use IRS 1040–ES to figure your estimated tax. Visit the IRS website at www.irs.gov and click on "Forms and Publications" to download a copy of the form and the publication that goes with it. The 1040-ES form includes a worksheet to help you figure your estimated tax and when payments are due.

Here's a useful table to help you determine if you need to make an estimated tax payment (based on when you expect to receive commission checks) and when you'll need to make them in order to avoid a penalty:

If you first have income on which you must pay estimated tax:	Make a payment by:	Make later installments by:
Before April 1	April 15	June 15 September 15 January 15 of next year
After March 31 and before June 1	June 15	September 15 January 15 of next year
After May 31 and before Sept. 1	September 15	January 15 of next year
After August 31	January 15 of next year	(None)

Employer Identification Numbers

An Employer Identification Number (EIN) is also known as a federal tax identification number, and is used to identify a business entity. Generally, businesses need an EIN, although as a sole proprietor you can also do business using your own Social Security number. Using EINs may be particularly smart for agents who have to share their tax ID numbers when receiving payments via MISC-1099 forms (see next section).

To figure out if the IRS requires you to have an EIN, take this quiz:

- Do you have employees?
- Do you operate your business as a corporation or a partnership?
- Do you file any of these tax returns: Employment, Excise, or Alcohol, Tobacco, and Firearms?
- Do you withhold taxes on income, other than wages, paid to a non-resident alien?
- Do you have a Keogh plan?
- Are you involved with any of the following types of organizations?
    - Trusts, except certain grantor-owned revocable trusts, IRAs, Exempt Organization Business Income Tax Returns
    - Estates
    - Real estate mortgage investment conduits
    - Non-profit organizations
    - Farmers' cooperatives
    - Plan administrators

If you answered "yes" to any of these questions, you will need to apply (either online at www.irs.gov) or by calling the IRS' Tele-TIN phone number at 1-800-829-4933.

1099-MISC Forms

Another tax issue that real estate agents face on a year-round basis is the management of 1099-MISC forms. These forms are sent to other real estate agents with whom you split commissions and to whom you've paid referral fees, and vice versa. Copies are sent directly to the IRS, which then reconciles them against your reported income when you file your taxes.

When 1099 payments exceed $600 in any given year (to a single entity), they must be reported to the IRS, unless the recipient's firm is incorporated (note: there are some new rules being developed at press time on this point, so be sure to talk to your CPA about it). That means the party will have to fill out a W-9 form. You'll then report that payment to the IRS via the 1099-MISC (and also sending one to the recipient). Should you get audited, you would have to pay a $100 penalty (plus interest) for every 1099 that wasn't reported.

To avoid such penalties, retain hard copies of all 1099s received throughout the tax year (which, for most, will run from January 1 to December 31), while also recording them in an electronic file for easy reference. Be sure to note any discrepancies between what you were paid and what the 1099 reflects, as the IRS will quickly inform you if your gross income doesn't match up with the 1099 total that it received for the year.

When and What to File

Knowing which tax forms to file—and when they need to be filed—is an important tax management step. Whether you're a new agent or an existing agent who hasn't yet nailed down a good tax management system, you'll want to follow this IRS chart to figure out exactly what's expected of you, and on what kind of timelines, throughout the year:

Tax Planning & Preparation

If you are liable for:	Use Form:	Deadline for filing:
Income tax	**1040** and **Schedule C** or **C-EZ**	15th day of 4th month after end of tax year.
Self-employment tax	**Schedule SE**	File with **Form 1040**
Estimated tax	**1040-ES**	15th day of 4th, 6th, and 9th months of tax year, and 15th day of 1st month after the end of tax year.
Social Security and Medicare taxes and income tax withholding	**941** **943** (Agriculture Taxes) **8109** (to make deposits)	April 30th, July 31, October 31, and January 31. See **IRS Publication 225** See **IRS Publication 15**
Providing information on social security and Medicare taxes and income tax withholding	**W-2** (to employee) **W-2** and **W-3** (to the Social Security Administration)	January 31 Last day of February (March 31 if filing electronically).
Federal Unemployment (FUTA) tax	**940** or **940-EZ** **8109** (to make deposits)	January 31. April 30, July 31, October 31, and January 31, but only if the liability for unpaid tax is more than $100.
Filing information returns for payments to nonemployees and transactions with other persons	See **Information Returns**	Forms **1099**-to the recipient by January 31 and to the IRS by February 28 (March 31 if filing electronically). Other forms— See the General Instructions for Forms **1099**,**1098**,**5498**, and **W-2G**.
Excise tax	See **Excise Taxes**	See the instructions to the form.
Partnership taxes	**1065**	April 15 following the close of the partnership's tax year if its accounting period is the calendar year. Fiscal Year Partnership—15th day of the 4th month following the close of its fiscal year. Provide each partner with **Schedule K-1 (Form 1065)**. See **Partnerships**

If you are liable for:	Use Form:	Deadline for filing:
S-Corporation taxes	**1120-S** **1120-W** (Estimated Taxes—Corporations Only and **8109**)	15th day of the 3rd month following the date the corporation's tax year ended as shown at the top of Form **1120S**. Calendar year—March 15, 2004. If due date falls on a Saturday, Sunday, or legal holiday, file on the next business day. If the S corporation election was terminated during the tax year, file Form **1120S** for the S corporation's short year by the due date (including extensions) of the C corporation's short year return. See **S-Corporations**
Corporate taxes	**1120** or **1120-A** **1120-W** (Estimated Taxes—Corporations Only and **8109**)	15th day of the 3rd month after the end of its tax year. New corporation filing a short-period return—15th day of the 3rd month after the short period ends. Corporation that has dissolved—15th day of the 3rd month after the date it dissolved. See **Corporations**
Limited Liability Company (LLC)	Only member of LLC is an individual—LLC income and expenses are reported on Form **1040**, Schedule **C**, **E**, or **F**. Only member of the LLC is a corporation, income and expenses are reported on the corporation's return, usually Form **1120** or Form **1120S**. Most LLCs with more than one member file a partnership return, Form **1065**. If you would rather file as a corporation, Form **8832** must be submitted. No Form **8832** is needed if filing as a partnership.	See **Publication 3402**

Hiring Help

Some agents choose to go it alone when it comes to tax preparation, while others swear by the services of a good accountant or tax advisor—either of which can even help you set up a financial software program. To find one, ask other agents who they use (since there are usually a few in any area that work often with real estate agents and brokers), use an online directory, or check with a local business group for a referral.

When one Illinois real estate agent made the move from a salaried job to full-time agent nine years ago, he grappled with a necessity that sends shivers down most agents' spines: paying estimated tax payments on time and in the appropriate amounts. Today, he socks away 25 percent of each commission check in a separate checking account, specifically for taxes.

"I pretend that money isn't there, until it's time to make my estimated payments," says the agent. Come April 15th (a double-whammy day for agents, when the previous year's tax returns and a first estimated payment for the current year are due), he doesn't have to scramble to dig up the funds. Along the way, this agent says one of the best tools that an agent can have is a good accountant who understands the tax challenges that small businesses and independent contractors face.

"No one wants to give their money away to an accountant, but you have to look at it like selling a home," he says. "It's like doing it by-owner or with a real estate agent, and we as an industry know which choice is the most beneficial for the consumer."

Just how much you'll pay an accountant to handle your taxes depends on where you're located and just how much of that person's time you'll require. Remember that a good tax professional will educate you as well as prepare any necessary returns and reports. Use the following guidelines to determine whether an accountant will pay off for you, and just what you can expect in return for your fees:

- For every $4,000 that a real estate agent nets during the year, $1,000 of it goes to the IRS.

- Typically, an expert professional for a self-employed, unincorporated agent will charge $200 to $500 to prepare a tax return. The average fee for a professional to prepare and submit a Form 1040 and state return with no itemized deductions is $176, the average fee for an itemized Form 1040 with Schedule A and a state tax return is $273, and the average fee for an itemized Form 1040 with Schedule C and a state tax return is $457, according to the National Society of Accountants' most recent numbers (2017).

- In return, the agent should expect face time with the expert, who will answer questions about taxes.

- The professional should also be available year-round to answer occasional quick questions free of charge by either phone or email.

- Additional assistance, such as calculating estimated tax payments due or tax planning will cost $150 to $250 per occurrence.

10 Tax Management Strategies for Real Estate Agents

1. Treat your business like a separate entity by maintaining a checking account and/or credit account dedicated only to business purposes.
2. Use QuickBooks, Freshbooks, Wave, NetSuite, or an Excel spreadsheet, to track income and expenses throughout the year.
3. Record all business expenses by entering them into your accounting system and maintaining hard copies of the receipts in a file.
4. Use a year-round budget to keep tabs on where you stand financially. Refer to it often, particularly when your income fluctuates significantly.

5. If your prior year Adjusted Gross Income (AGI) was $150,000 or less, you can avoid a penalty by paying either 90 percent of this year's income tax liability or 100 percent of your income tax liability from last year (dividing what you paid last year into four quarterly payments). If your prior year's AGI was greater than $150,000, then to avoid a penalty you'll need to pay either 90 percent of this year's income tax liability or 110 percent of last year's income tax liability.

6. When you split a commission with another agent, or pay out a referral fee, ask the recipient to fill out a W-9 form and issue 1099-MISC forms to those whom you pay out over $600 in any given year.

7. Set up a retirement account, find out what the upper contribution limits are, and start socking money away for your future, tax-free.

8. Hire a good tax advisor or accountant who understands the real estate business.

9. Check out a website like Quicken (www.quicken.com), Turbo-Tax (www.turbotax.com), or the H&R Block Tax Information Center (www.hrblock.com/tax-center) to learn about new tax changes that might affect you, and/or discuss them with your tax advisor.

10. Instead of ignoring potential tax problems, meet them head-on, deal with them and move on.

Getting Going

Most experts and agents agree that tracking expenses digitally during the year is the best way to get a handle on your taxes without having to deal with reams and reams of paper, receipt slips, and other distractions. Simply enter them into your system on a daily or weekly basis, then pull up the information to file your:

- Estimated tax payments
- Quarterly employment tax returns (for those agents who are incorporated)
- Annual federal tax returns
- Annual city and state tax returns

While some agents may still opt for the manual way of retaining receipts, a digital system will help you keep everything up to date and allow you to get an instant snapshot of your finances at any time, so that you're not scrambling through your car, purse, or basement for receipts and records. Commit to scanning your receipts into a software program on a weekly basis or enlist a system like Neat (www.neat.com) to do the receipt scanning and organizing work for you.

Maintain a diary of expenses, get everything into a digital format and update it as often as possible. And even if you do get behind, remember that rectifying the issue now—rather than later—is always a good idea. Then, use the experience as a lesson for next year and start focusing on year-round tax planning versus last-minute strategies to avoid the same challenges next year.

CHAPTER EIGHT

Personal and Professional Development

Becoming a successful real estate agent takes more than just passing pre-licensure and licensing exams and hanging your license on the wall of a broker's office. In fact, most agents will tell you that, unlike what it takes to become a doctor or attorney, the educational challenges in real estate are minimal. The hard part lies in turning that knowledge into actual business and, of course, commission checks. That's where the planning comes into play.

From this book, you've already learned how to create a business plan and marketing plan, and how to think and act like a business owner by addressing issues like incorporation and taxes. In this chapter, we'll take a look at personal and professional development that will help you either break into the industry or propel you to the next level. We'll discuss what it takes to stay on the leading edge while at the same time creating an enjoyable work and personal life—neither of which is easy to balance in today's hectic business environment.

We'll also look at some of the most popular ways to branch out and grow your business beyond just being a solo practitioner. That could mean forming a team, partnering with another agent, hiring help, or outsourcing work to virtual assistants who specialize in working with real estate agents. You'll also learn about some of the key designations that agents have after their names, find out how to get them yourself, and learn why they're valuable to agents.

Developing Professionally

Professional development in real estate goes beyond taking the continuing education courses that licensees are required to take every two years (individual states have their own requirements, so check with your state real estate commission or department of business for specifics). There are designations to earn, technology tools to invest in, social networking platforms to sign up for, workshops to attend, online classes to participate in, and a slew of industry-related publications to pore over—and that's just at the macro level. At your local level, you'll also need to stay up to date on market knowledge, consumer preferences, housing trends, and other important aspects of the real estate industry.

Now, what you <u>don't</u> want to do is spend too much time or money on professional development opportunities that won't pay off. Because you're not punching a clock or being closely supervised, it's easy to get thrown off track by a 3-day out-of-town seminar, and then come back to an empty client pipeline. To avoid wasting your time, both new and existing agents should:

- **Ask past attendees** exactly what they gained from attending the course, online educational offering, or seminar. Find out whether or not it helped them grow their business, expand their professional knowledge, and/or meet new contacts in the industry. If it did none of those, don't waste your time or money.

- **Find out what the course or seminar covers**, and decide if they cover areas where you need help. For example:
  - A new agent would probably benefit from a basic half-day class on how to turn online leads into paying customers.
  - An existing agent who has been in the business for two years would probably want a more advanced or specific

half-day course on "How to maximize your sphere of influence to take your sales up a notch."

- **Go online** for courses and professional development opportunities, and for feedback on them. Real estate agents are a pretty open group that likes to share the best and worst of their experiences.

As a real estate agent, you'll be required to take certain continuing education courses to maintain your license. Each state has different requirements, so check with your local Board of REALTORS or real estate commission for details.

In Florida, for example, real estate brokers and salespersons are required to complete 14 hours of CE every two years after their first license renewal—and prior to their license expiration date—according to the Florida Real Estate Commission (FREC). As of 2017, three of the 14 CE required hours must include an Ethics and Business Practices course approved by FREC.

Agents can also turn to state and national REALTOR conventions, where top industry experts often hold educational sessions, a number of which have been approved for continuing education credit. The best way to find the right course or event is by consulting with other agents and brokers for recommendations. Get your hands on the books, online materials, and the coursework. Browse through them before signing up, always keeping an eye out for readability, accuracy, thoroughness, and relevance to your business.

CE courses go beyond just fulfilling a requirement. They can also help agents keep up with a constantly changing marketplace where recent developments in laws relating to condominiums, timesharing, building code violations, pool safety regulations, and federal income taxes are important. Also key are the disclosure requirements and legal liability associated with polybutylene plumbing pipes, toxic mold, radon, Megan's law, brown fields, and lead-based paint; and fair housing, financing trends, automated underwriting, and valuation and contracts—not to mention the all-important ethics that NAR and all state real estate regulatory bodies place a high emphasis on. Here are a few great ways to make the most out of the required CE experience, and how to apply the knowledge you've learned in your own business setting:

- Before choosing a course or format, talk to a few agents and brokers to find out which courses and formats they've used in the past, then base your decision on these positive or negative experiences.

- Instead of taking the cheap and quick way out, opt for a course that has true take-away value and additional modules like finance or ethics that you can apply to your own business.

- Know your learning style, and choose a format that matches it. Do you learn by the book? Do you prefer an interactive, classroom setting? Would you rather take an online course?

- View CE as an opportunity to learn about changes to the license, your state real estate commission's rules, and recent developments along with other laws relating to real estate.

- Translate the words that are flat on the course page into three-dimensional strategies by asking yourself: How can I use this in my business? How can I apply this newfound knowledge to my day-to-day routine?

- While taking the course, look for ways to move the abstract information on that flat page into counseling, and listing and sales presentations.

- If you're taking CE in a classroom setting, look for an instructor who encourages classroom participation. Many agents learn just as much from the examples and experiences of the group as from the material itself.

- Come to class ready to focus on the material and contribute to the group discussions. If possible, read the material before the class begins to get a head start.

- Finally, look at CE as an opportunity rather than an obligation and look for tidbits of information and knowledge that you can apply in your own business.

As a new entrepreneur, you'll need to balance professional and personal development with your daily work obligations. While there are certain courses that you will have to complete to keep your license active, there are only so many hours in a day for the rest of the opportunities. With the proliferation of online learning you may find yourself bombarded with options. Research them carefully, selecting only those that will truly add value to your career, rather than wasting your time on the options that sap your finances and time.

Growing Your Business

There comes a time in every good agent's life when there simply aren't enough hours in the day to do all of the business that comes your way. It's every new agent's dream scenario, but it can quickly turn into a nightmare for the existing agent who suddenly finds himself working 24/7, trying to close deals, show homes, create marketing materials, answer email, post social media updates, and submit listing materials to the MLS.

To keep your business growing, you have several ways to alleviate the stress and strive for higher sales and more closed transactions. Here's a look at the five basic choices, and the pros and cons of each:

- Hire a part- or full-time licensed assistant

  Pro: You can almost immediately begin to unload all tasks (even those related to the real estate transaction) to this new person.

  Con: You become an employer and manager, and you may be training your next competitor.

- Hire a part- or full-time unlicensed assistant

Pro: The new person can handle all of your administrative tasks, such as taking phone calls, checking email, and filing.

Con: You become an employer and manager, and in most states this employee cannot handle any tasks directly related to the real estate transaction.

- Pair up with another agent in your office

    Pro: If the match works well (and in many cases it does), the two of you can share all aspects of your workloads, and even cover for each other when one person is sick or on vacation.

    Con: You'll need to work out an amicable compensation split when sharing deals, and you may not always find that "best match" partner on the first try.

- Form a team

    Pro: You can spread the work around among your team, which would likely be made up of a buyer specialist, listing specialist, transaction coordinator, and administrative assistant.

    Con: Though a popular choice for today's agents, teams take time and care to cultivate and grow. Finding the right team members can be a challenge, but when you hit on the right mix you'll be more apt to achieve higher sales and overall success.

- Outsource some of the work to a virtual assistant (either on-site or off-site)

    Pro: You're not an employer, since these professionals operated as independent contractors on a 1099 basis.

    Con: Since this person probably won't work in your office, he or she works under little supervision. Also, virtual assistants without specific real estate training may lack the industry knowledge needed to perform work quickly and accurately.

Personal and Professional Development

Eight Team-Building Tips

1. Look for an assistant, partner, or team member whose strengths and weaknesses complement your own.

2. Check with your individual company's guidelines and state Real Estate Commission rules for hiring assistants or forming teams before making any decisions about expanding your business.

3. When pairing up with other agents or unlicensed assistants, look not only at the person's real estate skills and knowledge, but also at their communication and people skills.

4. Talk to your broker or office manager for suggestions on finding a partner, team, or assistant who will be most compatible with your own skills.

5. Work out an amicable pay scale or compensation plan that works for everyone involved. A team of three agents, for example, may opt to split expenses and commissions three ways.

6. Start out slow by delegating time-consuming tasks like database management and follow-up calls that steal your time away from working directly with homebuyers and sellers.

7. Once you find the right person or team members, set your sights not only on increasing your sales, but also on freeing up your own personal time.

8. Don't let one bad choice of assistants or partners ruin your chances of multiplying your success. If at first you don't succeed, try, try again!

Going Virtual

Virtual and remote assistants who work from their own offices and who can handle myriad non-core tasks for professionals have become a popular option for business owners. If hiring employees, paying payroll taxes, and managing others aren't of interest, then a virtual assistant may be just the ticket.

Here are some clues that a virtual assistant might be the right solution for your growing real estate business:

- You need help on a per-project basis that doesn't warrant a full- or part-time staff member.

- You need more time to sell property.

- You aren't focusing on your core competencies (sales, consultations, investments, etc).

- You have limited space available in your office for additional staff members.

- You are totally overwhelmed in your business and can't keep up with the details.

- You're willing to delegate and give up some control over non-core tasks to an off-site assistant.

- You're a people person who doesn't like hanging around the office doing paperwork.

- You're a brand-new agent who has experienced early success and is in need of assistance, but you're not ready to hire full-time help.

- You don't have the time to handle all of the necessary marketing tasks that need to be done.

- You're not technology oriented, and would rather have someone else handle that tasks like updating accounting software, creating virtual tours, and posting social media updates.

- You know what needs to be done, but you just don't have time to do it all.

- After months of training your last on-site assistant, he or she became your competitor.

Teamwork Makes the Dream Work

In a recent Real Trends blog, I wrote about how family-owned businesses can bring relatives closer together and allow them to work side-by-side all day, every day. But they also present issues that non-family entities don't have to work through. For Greg Johnston of Keller Williams Realty East Idaho and one of the franchises' top-selling agents, working with his older brother Mike Johnston (office broker who doesn't list or sell) and their father, Jim Johnston, has proven to be a magical combination.

"People often say to me, 'Greg, I'm surprised that you can work with family, because a lot of people can't do that,'" says Johnston, who has been working with his father for the last 19 years. "But we've found a formula which works in an industry where not all family teams get along, and where some just wind up going out on their own."

Here's how they do it:

1. **They check their egos at the door.** Being selfish or self-centered doesn't cut it in a family business, where everyone has to pull their weight and be "in it" for the right reasons. This is particularly important in real estate, where all members of the family tend to have the same sphere of influence to pull from. "We're working together, so it's not about any one person," says Johnston. "When one of us wins, we all win."

2. **They collaborate a lot.** Open lines of communication are critical in a family business, where close relationships between team members can be both a blessing and a curse. The Johnstons regularly bounce ideas off one another ("Hey, who are you meeting with this afternoon?" and "Who's covering the office this morning?") and coordinate their activities in a way that benefits everyone. "Good communication really goes far in the team environment," he says.

3. **They sell themselves as a "package" deal.** In today's real estate market, consumers like instant responses from people who know their stuff. Because their knowledge is cloned across multiple family members, the Johnstons often use the pitch: "Hey, you're getting all of us for the price of one." So, where a seller may sign her listing paperwork with Greg, the next day that seller could find herself working directly with Jim to set up an inspection.

4. **They're not afraid to crack jokes at their own expense.** When people ask Johnston where he gets his business from, he likes to joke that "he stole all of his dad's business," and that's how he generates his leads. "They called my dad first," he says, "and when he wasn't available, I started working with them."

Setting Priorities

If you haven't caught onto it yet, setting priorities is absolutely critical when you're operating as a small businessperson in a commission-based environment. Without predetermined parameters to help you maximize your time, it's very easy to get caught up in day-to-day tasks that take up too much of your time while not producing enough income. In real estate, for example, the following activities tend to consume an agent's time, yet aren't always the most profitable use of his or her time:

- Socializing with other agents and brokers in your office over coffee
- Socializing with other agents and brokers from <u>outside</u> offices
- Using Facebook, Twitter and Instagram for non-business activities
- Attending association and trade meetings that may not have a direct impact on your business

- Giving advice to homeowners and homebuyers who have no intention of using your services in exchange for a fee

- Browsing the Internet and/or MLS systems in search of area information, new and expired listings, or other "chance" opportunities that may or may not turn into actual business for you

Granted, some of these activities can produce business, but only if used in moderation. If you don't have a way of outsourcing some of the more mundane tasks to another individual, you'll definitely want to start setting both personal and business priorities. In return, you can truly expect to make the best use of your time while still being able to lead a satisfying life outside of work.

Time for Yourself

One Massachusetts real estate agent with 28 years of experience in the business has, over time, mastered the art of building a successful business without sacrificing his personal life. Rewind back to the 1980s, however, and he says he was just another agent who was burning the candle at both ends. That was, until he realized that his children and spouse needed him just as much as his business did, if not more.

"I found out a long time ago that I had to plan my personal life first and my business life second," says the agent, who is proud to say he never missed a parent-teacher conference, soccer game, or dance recital. Setting those boundaries also helped his business, which has grown steadily over the last three decades. "The formula is simple: the more you schedule your time—both personal and business—the more money you will make," he says. "The balance plays a key factor in that success because when you're working you will really work; and when you're playing, you will really play."

One agent in Illinois says setting priorities is especially important in the real estate industry, where seemingly legitimate tasks can take all day to complete. Without a boss looking over your shoulder, urging you on, you can easily allocate too much time to those obligations that do little to advance your career.

"I've seen a lot of agents spend too much time on stuff that takes them away from what they really need to be doing: lead generation and business development," he says. "In this business, the most successful agents have a razor-sharp focus on three or four 'big rocks,' and they work on those, in priority order. The other tasks have to get done too, but they can usually be handled later, after the most important tasks are off your desk."

Effective Time Management Tactics for Real Estate Agents

- Outsource tasks that you don't have the time and/or expertise to complete.

- Finish projects early to reduce deadline stress and lighten your own workload.

- Know your own limits, or risk the possibility of burnout. If you're hitting overload, for example, take a few hours off for a walk in the park or a good workout. Have lunch with a friend.

- Strive for organization by taking time at the end of the workday to get ready for the next day.

- Use an agenda and follow it; delete tasks as you complete them.

- Divide up your time by deciding just how much to spend on business development, personal needs, and family/friend obligations.

- Allow for flexibility in your schedule, and surround yourself with reliable friends, family, and co-workers who can help out in the time of need.

- Make it clear to clients that you are not an around-the-clock agent, but that you are indeed a capable and competent professional who works set hours.

Start Now

I'm hoping that this book has already given you a good idea of how to create a roadmap for your business, develop your professional self, set priorities, and create both marketing and business plans. From that vantage point, the best personal development steps you can take right now require just a calendar and agenda to get started. Using whatever mechanism works best for you, it's time to:

- Jot down all of your personal appointments (including workouts, gatherings with friends and family events).

- Add in floor time, time spent monitoring your office's incoming Internet leads, training sessions, and other broker-related activities that you're asked to partake in.

- Block out time every day or week for important business tasks like lead generation, farming, and customer follow up.

- Then, carve out areas of the day and/or week where business appointments and meetings would fit best.

- When calls come in for showings, listing appointments or other obligations, refer to your calendar before saying "yes."

One real estate coach calls this strategy "time blocking" and says that to make it work you'll need to set certain appointments—particularly the personal ones—as "unalterable."

"Many agents will make the time for lead generation, but when something comes up it's usually the family or personal time that suffers as a result," says the coach. "New agents have an especially hard time blocking out a Saturday afternoon to spend with their kids, then preserving that time when someone calls for a listing appointment. It's very difficult to pass that up."

By establishing boundaries, setting priorities, and laying down the law right now, both new and existing agents will find themselves in much more control of a career that can easily run 24 hours a day, seven days a week, if you let it.

Sticking to this routine may be harder than it sounds during your first year or two in business—since you'll likely be more focused on getting commission checks than getting to the gym for that spin class or Crossfit workout on time—but try it anyway. By taking time for yourself and your family and/or friends when you can and setting priorities, you'll have a much better handle on the situation. As a bonus, you'll also avoid the burnout that many new and existing agents grapple with on a daily basis.

CHAPTER NINE

Long-Term Planning

It's not unusual for real estate agents to backburner their own needs as they focus on handling the day-to-day real estate tasks, keeping those commission checks coming in, and managing a stable of new and existing clients. Because no employer is socking away money for them in a retirement account, providing health insurance benefits or giving them stock options, agents who overlook these and other personal aspects of their businesses can find themselves in trouble down the road.

To determine if you're one of these agents, answer "yes" or "no" to the following questions and check your score at the end of the quiz:

1. Do I know how much I'm saving and spending every year?
2. Am I using a household budget to manage my money?
3. Am I investing for my financial future?
4. Do I have the proper choices in my retirement or 401(k) plan?
5. Do I have health insurance coverage for myself and my family (if applicable)?
6. Do I have life insurance?
7. Do I have a means of providing long-term care for elderly family members, if necessary?
8. If I have children, have I established a means of investing for their college education?

9. Have I sat down with a financial planner within the last five years to discuss my "nest egg" and other relevant financial topics?
10. Do I know how much of my annual income needs to be saved in order to maintain my standard of living in retirement?

Scoring:

8–10 "yes" answers: You're well on your way to having a solid plan in place for your future.

5–7 "yes" answers: You're getting there, but you'll definitely want to look at some of the "no" areas to see where you can beef up your long-term planning.

1–4 "yes" answers: Time to take a step back from your day-to-day workload and do some long-term financial planning for yourself and your family.

If your score wasn't up to par, you're not alone. Most financial professionals know that inadequate long-term planning is endemic among small business owners, including real estate agents. "The biggest challenge for agents is making time for themselves to create—and then commit—to a business, financial, and life plan," says one financial planner, "and to understand how their current work ties into their goals."

That's because successful real estate agents tend to have a consistent internal wiring that allows them to prosper, regardless of market conditions or the economy. They react quickly, focus on client needs and even place their clients' needs ahead of their own. Unfortunately, these business strengths can also be weaknesses.

"Real estate agents tend to subordinate their own business, financial, and life planning matters to the practice of real estate," says the planner, who himself is a former real estate professional who often works with agents and brokers, helping them create long-term plans for financial success. In doing so, he's noticed that real estate agents postpone personal financial planning meetings at least five times more often than his firm's non-real estate clients—mainly because they're spending time on listing presentations, open houses, web-based marketing, and farming for new prospects.

On the bright side, he says real estate agents have access to significant benefits that other small business owners may not have at their fingertips, including the ability to:

- Build a long-term referral business to ensure long-term value for their practices
- Distinguish themselves strategically by creating a network of resources for their clients
- Be well-versed in investment real estate, and serve a niche that is sorely lacking
- Invest in real estate, and take advantage of discounts, rebates, and referral fees
- Be aggressive in their retirement planning
- Scale their businesses up (or, down) while keeping a tight lid on expenses
- Relocate their businesses fairly easily, if so desired

The irony is that many successful agents who have been in the business a reasonable amount of time desperately look forward to cutting back on the time spent working, or even getting out of the business entirely. Yet, very few know what that looks like financially. "Very few people (and even fewer agents) understand the financial capital needed to maintain their existing standard of living during retirement," says the financial planner, "and even fewer understand the impact of taxes, inflation, social security, or working part time."

To avoid falling into that trap, real estate agents need to begin their long-term planning well before they're no longer willing or able to work. The longer the time to financial independence, the more options and alternatives the agent has. "I've seen too many times that an agent and his/her spouse, ages 55 or older, are on track to outlive their money because they failed to plan," says the financial planner. "There is no better hedge to successful planning than planning as far in advance of retirement as possible."

Early Steps

To create an effective long-term plan for personal and financial success in real estate, you'll want to revisit some of the basic business planning concepts covered in the earlier chapters of this book. Here are the key steps you should be taking:

- Make sure you go into the business with your eyes open and with the support of your significant other and/or the other important people in your life.

- Create a business and marketing plan that is attainable, and that creates accountability.

- Work with a professional to get a snapshot of your financial condition (including key components like: assets, cash flow, and estate planning).

- Make sure all assets are optimized based on your own unique risk tolerance (defined as the degree of uncertainty that an investor can handle should a negative change impact his or her portfolio's value).

- Control business and household expenses by tracking the last 12 months' expenses, and by setting a budget going forward.

- Align your current financial condition, personal financial goals, and business planning objectives.

- Provide for an appropriate level of reserves to launch your business and to ride out market swings and seasonality.

- Measure your success and adjust accordingly.

- Take care of yourself.

Long-Term Planning

Once an agent has experienced success in the industry—and starts to bring in a reasonable level of discretionary income—exploring appropriate retirements plans and other strategies to defer or reduce taxes becomes critical. With a retirement plan, for example, you not only can sock away pre-tax dollars, but you can also reduce tax liabilities by setting up and funding such accounts. Here's a look at the three popular retirement options for agents:

SIMPLE-IRA

Key advantage: Salary reduction plan with little administrative paperwork.

Eligibility: Any business with 100 or fewer employees that does not currently maintain any other retirement plan.

Your responsibilities: Set up by completing IRS Form 5304-SIMPLE or 5305-SIMPLE. No employer tax filing required. The bank or financial institution handles the bulk of the paperwork.

Maximum annual contribution per participant: Employee—$13,000 for 2019 (or $16,000 for those aged 50 or older, thanks to the $3,000 "catch-up contribution" option). Employer—Either match employee contributions dollar for dollar up to 3 percent of compensation or contribute 2 percent of each eligible employee's compensation.

Minimum employee coverage: Must be offered to all employees who have earned at least $5,000 in the previous two years.

SEP-IRA

Key advantage: Easy to set up and maintain.

Eligibility: Any business with one or more employees.

Your responsibilities: Set up a plan by completing IRS Form 5305-SEP. No employer tax filing required.

Maximum annual contribution per participant: For 2019, the lesser amount of 25 percent of compensation or $56,000.

Minimum employee coverage: Must be offered to all employees who are at least 21 years of age, employed by the business for three of the last five years, and who earned at least $400 in a year.

401 (k)

Key advantage: Permits employee to contribute more than in other options.

Eligibility: Any business with one or more employee.

Your responsibilities: Consult with a financial institution or employee benefit provider, as there is no "model form" used to establish a plan. The plan requires an annual filing of IRS Form 5500 and special testing to ensure that it does not discriminate in favor of highly-compensated employees.

Maximum annual contribution per participant: Employee aged 49 and under, $19,000 (for 2019) and an additional $6,000 allowed for workers over 50. There is a total contribution limit (employer plus employee) of $56,000.

Minimum employee coverage: Must be offered to all employees at least 21 years of age who worked at least 1,000 hours during the previous year.

Before selecting a retirement plan, you'll want to discuss your strategy with a financial advisor or accountant who can fill you in on any new details, requirements, or drawbacks to certain plans.

Strategizing for Success

When you're reviewing your retirement options with a qualified advisor, you'll also want to tap his or her knowledge on how to:

- Create a comprehensive plan that aligns your business and financial matters with your own personal goals.

- Plan seriously for events that would negatively impact planning, like long term care, disability, and certainly death. (How will the ones left behind be provided for?)

- Focus on the end game by asking yourself:
  - What will happen when I leave the business?
  - What type of business succession and continuity planning should I have in place to optimize the future value of the practice I've built?
  - What type of legacy in the business do I want to leave, and how will I get there?

- Now, think further into the future by asking yourself:
  - How do I want to have my estate distributed when I pass away?
  - Who will I enrich, and how will I go about doing this?
  - Is my estate plan appropriate, and does it account for the future value of my assets?
  - Have I created a plan that will pass almost everything to my beneficiaries, and that minimizes estate taxes and probate costs?
  - Have these documents been reviewed recently?
  - Is the titling of my assets appropriate for my estate plan?

Once you've tackled these "big picture" items, drill down on a few key financial planning points. If you're working with a financial planner, this person will probably go over each of these components. If you're doing it on your own, here are the aspects of your personal and business life that should be addressed:

- Current situation, risk tolerance, time horizon, and personal and financial goals

- Cash flow
- Retirement planning
- Retirement distribution
- Investment planning
- Tax strategies
- Estate planning (or wealth preservation for high-net worth individuals)
- Education planning
- Special needs (disabilities, senior dependents)
- Risk management (death, disability, long term care)
- Survivorship
- Accumulation needs (weddings, vacation home, boat)
- Educational needs
- Business succession and continuity
- Immediate cash needs (reserves)

Expect to spend about $1,500–$2,500 (give or take a few dollars, depending your specific needs and where you're located) for a financial planner's assistance with this process. Also expect to meet with the professional a few times (either in person, on the phone, or using videoconferencing) to iron out the details and finalize the plan. Here's a look at how one financial planner divides up that time when working with clients, many of whom collaborate with him via phone, videoconferencing, Facetime, etc.:

- First meeting: Preliminary data gathering—mostly questions for the agent about family, goals, anxieties, current assets and cash flow, and current estate plan.

- Second meeting: If there appears to be both a need and a match, then he goes into comprehensive data gathering (qualitative and quantitative) of statistics, documents, and dreams.

- Third meeting: Preliminary plan design for all relevant areas of planning, based on the client needs. For example, a couple with no children doesn't need education planning.

- Fourth meeting: Testing suitable concepts and strategies that meet the agent's objectives.

- Fifth meeting: Final plan presentation.

- Sixth meeting: Implementation of the plan, then a periodic, scheduled review of the plan (generally on a semi-annual basis, with quarterly reports provided to the agent).

Other Considerations

There are a few more elements that you won't want to leave out of your long-term business plan. Along with the must-haves already discussed, here are a few other building blocks that you'll want to take into consideration:

- **Health Insurance:** Unless they're fortunate enough to have a spouse with a full-time job and benefits, most real estate agents grapple with the issue of health insurance coverage at some point during their career. Knowing this, many of the larger real estate franchises now offer a selection of healthcare plans (through third parties) to their agents. Explore your options and shop around to find the best plan for you and your family.

- **Other Types of Insurance:** Having suitable property and casualty coverage is equally as important, especially for real estate agents. Umbrella insurance offers the highest ratio of benefit to cost, and is a good way to protect an estate. Life insurance is another important planning tool and generally comprises three phases: Insurance to provide for the ongoing existence and support of the family (lower and middle class), self-insurance (upper class), and insurance as an estate planning strategy (affluent).

- **College educations:** As a parent, the world is your oyster right now when it comes to college savings. Families can plan to cover all, most, or some of their children's anticipated costs, while grandparents and other family members can be rallied to do the same. There are also grants, scholarships, state prepaid, and 529 plans, among others. "There are some types of resources for most people for most circumstances," says the financial planner, who adds that planning is the key to success in this area. Some of the trickier aspects of college include what school (or more like, what tuition) to target, in state or out, room and board or stay at home, and the future cost of college. There are so many variables that it might make sense to have a progressive plan in place, with the 529 plan being one of the best choices. You can learn more about college savings options online at: www.savingforcollege.com.

- **Real Estate Investments:** With the stock market fluctuating over the last few years, real estate has remained a viable investment option for agents and other investors. For those who aren't ready to go out and buy property, Real Estate Investment Trusts (REITS, which are companies that invest in real estate or real estate-related assets) are a good way to hold this asset for the more conservative and smaller investor.

- **Long-term care (LTC) for elderly parents:** With the nation's elderly population growing, LTC has become a hot issue for everyone, yet most people have no plan in place to address the issues of a protracted illness. If in need of a rehabilitative, therapeutic, diagnostic, maintenance, or personal care service in a setting other than an acute care unit of a hospital (such as a nursing home or your own residence), these costs would have to be provided by your personal assets. According to the Federal Long Term Care Insurance Program, the likelihood of needing long-term care and the financial consequences of it are surprisingly high:
    - Roughly, half of all persons over 65 will spend some time in a nursing home.

- The average stay is approximately 2½ years.
- Nursing home stays (semiprivate room) cost $91,615 annually.
- Assisted living facilities cost $47,064 per year.
- Home health care aides cost $32,760 annually.
- Medicare covers only about 2 percent of these costs.

As you can see, incorporating LTC into any long-term planning that you do as an agent means not having to deal with larger financial consequences down the road. Take the time to plan ahead today.

Investing in Real Estate

Armed with an inherent and acquired knowledge of real estate and how the buying and selling process works, real estate brokers and agents can make very good candidates for commercial and residential real estate investment. Making the option particularly attractive are the nation's rising property values, which have helped investors post significant gains on their real estate portfolios in a short period of time. Disenchanted with the stock market and enticed by low mortgage interest rates, many investors have turned to real estate as an investment option. And while the housing market downturn of 2005 left some homeowners and investors licking their wounds, real estate remains a good, long-term investment for just about anyone.

Take one broker, who started working for Century 21 in 1989 and immediately began adding properties to his own portfolio. Back then, getting financed was a challenge, so the agent went after anything with owner financing that he could get his hands on, namely condominiums and single-family homes. "I bought the stuff that wasn't selling," says the agent, who today buys tracts of land for residential development. He works together with partners who put up the cash for the purchases, and then handles the entire process from start to finish.

"It works out tremendously well," says the agent. Whether he's buying a one-bedroom condo or a 40-acre tract of land, the key to success is to lay out a plan before buying. He also takes into consideration the different demands for each type of property. For vacant land, grass must be cut and taxes paid long before any development is complete. When buying a duplex, however, the agent knows he'll have two rental incomes coming in, right out of the block.

Like any good agent would, this investor also relies on his own industry experience and sheer instinct to help during the decision-making process. "Very often," he adds, "I can just look at a piece of property and the ideas start popping into my head."

The Long-Term View

There's no time like the present to take a long-term view of your real estate career and not only create a business plan for developing business, but that provides a stable future for yourself and your family. Getting there requires a well-rounded view of your own finances, your financial goals, and a measurement of what kind of risk you're willing to take to get there. Here are some examples for various stages of the business:

New Real Estate Agent: Fresh out of real estate school, a new agent may lack the financial means and wherewithal to create a complete financial plan, but that doesn't mean she can't:

- Shop around for a good health insurance plan for herself
- Shell out a small fee to start a SEP-IRA plan for her future
- Purchase a term life insurance policy

Agent with Two Years of Experience: An agent with two years under his belt and a child who is six years away from college will want to take all of the steps mentioned above, plus:

- Sit down with a financial planner to incorporate more elements into a long-term plan for personal financial success

- Start a 529 or other college savings plan
- Consider a retirement plan that allows for larger contributions (such as a 401(k) plan)
- Think about investing in real estate as part of his overall investment portfolio
- Factor in other issues like long-term care, investments accounts (such as mutual funds or individual stocks)

Agent with 10 Years of Experience: Depending on the agent's financial situation, and just how much planning she's done along the way, this agent will want to take all of the steps outlined above, plus:

- Consider any key tax strategies that will allow her to keep more income
- Meet annually with her financial planner to make adjustments to the long-term plan
- Regularly review all insurance policies to make sure they're current and aligned with her life goals and financial position

When planning for the long-term, there are a few important matters to keep in mind, whether you're a brand-new agent, or one who has been in the industry for 10 years. They are:

- Keep an eye on taxes; there are very good strategies for reducing taxes that business owners can use legitimately.
- Increase contributions not only to retirement plans, but also to fund other parts of the plan (such as insurance and education).
- Always keep your personal goals in mind, and tie your financial decisions in with your overall financial plan.
- Review and refresh your plan every three to four years, or when a major event of life change occurs (a new baby, a marriage, a divorce, etc.).

- As your business grows and prospers, make sure that your current plan accounts for the additional cash flow and minimizes taxes.

As you work your way through the various components involved with long-term planning for success, remember that "one size fits all" probably won't work. By first examining your own business aspirations, life goals, and responsibilities, then leveraging them with a customized, comprehensive plan, your chances of achieving those goals will increase exponentially.

"During my last 50 first-time meetings with prospective clients, the outcome was different for each," says the financial planner we heard from earlier in this book. "There are some common problem areas (estate planning, cash flow, expenses, retirement planning, retirement distribution, coordination of investments, and suitability of investments), but because of each agent's unique risk tolerance, time horizon, current situation, and goals, the advice and plans are always very different."

To those agents who have yet to consider the bigger picture, he says, "start planning now." The longer you wait, the fewer options that may be available, based on tax law changes, age limitations, and other issues beyond your control. The sooner you start, the more certainty and control you will have of the outcome.

"Financial planning gives people a great sense of comfort and freedom. Even for those whose trajectory appears that they may outlive their money, it gives them a sense of awareness, the ability to make adjustments, and a little more control," says one planner. "Real estate agents thrive on control and unbeknown to most, a financial and/or business plan is a roadmap to ultimate control: financial independence."

Start Planning Today

Throughout this book, I've given you solid advice, reasons and action tips for creating a comprehensive success map for your real estate career, no matter what stage of the game you're at. Remember that a business plan is not only critical to the success of a new business, but it can also help existing business owners stay on track and hone the future of their businesses.

And while it is certainly possible to start and run a real estate business <u>without</u> a plan, the chances for success improve greatly when you have a detailed blueprint to follow. Plus, the very act of creating the plan forces you to think through issues that might otherwise be overlooked—or handled on the fly—such as:

1. Who are my competitors?
2. How big is my target market?
3. How can I reach this target market?
4. What would happen if I were to expand my farm area by 500 houses?
5. How much business would I lose if I took a 2-week vacation?
6. How much cash flow does my business generate?
7. What is my company's profit and loss?
8. What do I need to do to earn an additional $50,000 in commissions each year?
9. How much should I allocate for advertising?
10. How can I find someone to help me serve my growing client base?
11. What kind of marketing works best in my area?
12. How can I put mobile apps, social, and other tech tools to good use in my business?
13. I don't have a huge sphere of influence, but can I use online leads to start building my business <u>today</u>?
14. How can I minimize my tax obligations?
15. How will I pay for my child's college education?
16. When can I stop working and retire?

These and other elements can be incorporated into a comprehensive business plan that puts your career heads and tails above the rest. "One mistake many small business owners make is creating a business plan because they are told they need one, and then completely forgetting about it. Once you have business plan created, consider it an internal tool you use on an ongoing basis in your business, updating it as necessary so it remains current," *The Balance* points out. "Remember that the most effective small business plans are those that are used as a living document in the business to help guide decisions and keep your business on track."

So, while many other agents may plod along, wondering where their next commission check is coming, you'll already know the answer to that question because you've thought through all of the essentials of running a business. There's no time like the present to take your business off autopilot and shake things up a bit with a few good planning sessions. Good luck!

APPENDIX A
Sample Business Plans

When developing your business plan, you'll probably fall into one of two camps:

- You're a new agent who needs a roadmap for success.
- You're an existing agent (with two or more years of experience in the field) and you either need to develop your first plan, or tweak one for maximum effectiveness.

In this section, we'll look at two sample business plans. The first focuses on the new agent who has already hung her license at a broker's office and is working hard to get to that first sale. The second centers on an agent who wants more out of his existing business. Use these sample plans as a guide for creating your own success strategies, but remember there are many variations to business plans and you'll probably need to tailor the format around your own business.

Sample Business Plan #1: New Agent

SUMMARY
Executive Summary:
Rhonda Jones is a new residential real estate agent who passed her licensing exam and hung her license with ABC Realty in Allentown, Pa. Armed with a limited amount of sales knowledge and several years

of experience as an office manager at a small industrial firm, Jones has resided in Allentown for 15 years and has a vast network of friends and family in the region. Having worked in an office for a number of years, she's tech savvy and knows how to use business software, platforms, and applications. Her knowledge of the real estate industry is limited, although she is familiar with the communities where she'll be working.

Business Concept: Jones will work with homebuyers and sellers in the residential real estate industry. Working on a 50/50 commission split with her broker, Jones will charge the going commission rate of 6 percent for her services (note that this is a negotiable fee that can't be "set"), splitting the fee with the cooperating broker. Using a combination of farming, floor time at her broker's office, canvassing of neighborhoods, and various advertising methods, Jones will list homes for sale and work with buyers, helping find the home of their dreams in exchange for a commission.

Current Situation: Jones has yet to list or sell a home, and is currently in the process of networking with her friends, family, colleagues, and new acquaintances to get the word out about her business. By helping existing agents staff their open houses, she's made some buyer contacts and has shown a few homes in the area to interested new buyers (none of whom have made offers yet).

Key Success Factors: Jones is very familiar with her area and knowledgeable about the many different neighborhoods within that area. She has a large network of potential clients and makes use of apps, Facebook, Instagram, and real estate software.

Key Challenges: Jones lacks an in-depth knowledge of her local real estate market in terms of its size, number of existing and new home sales, and related information. She's also just learning how the cooperation between brokers works in the industry.

Financial Situation/Needs: Jones has a 6-month cash reserve that she's hoping will see her through the first few lean months in the real estate business. With just a few weeks under her belt as an agent, Jones has to close one or more deals within the next six months in order to sustain herself in her current, full-time position as an agent. She has no dependents, so she can take a slightly higher risk for the next six months to a year without putting anyone (except herself) in financial jeopardy. Jones has a small retirement fund—started at her previous job—which she plans to begin funding again when it's financially feasible. She also has health insurance (via the COBRA system) from her last employer, which she pays for herself.

VISION

Vision Statement: By acting as a facilitator during the home buying and selling process for people in her area, and by providing the highest possible service levels to those individuals, Jones will create a business that supports her lifestyle while also allowing her to save for her future. To make that happen, Jones will continually hone her professional skills through training; earn the appropriate designations; and operate in a fair, ethical manner.

MARKET ANALYSIS

The Overall Market: Using her local MLS and various real estate research sites as references, Jones knows that the existing home market is healthy in the Lehigh Valley region of Pennsylvania. Homes priced $200,000 to $350,000 are in highest demand, along with any available affordable housing.

Changes in the Market: Like most of the nation, the Lehigh Valley area has experienced typical property appreciation rates over the last two years. While much of the housing stock is 50-plus years old in the region, there has been an influx of new home construction that's supported by job growth at many of the region's larger manufacturers and distribution facilities.

Target Market and Customers: With her office situated in the city of Allentown, Jones has chosen to focus her efforts on the city itself, plus nearby suburban areas like Bath, Trexlertown, Macungie, and other, largely residential communities. Her target customers include first-time homebuyers, relocating professionals (based on her company's national referral database), and individuals and families who are "moving up" into larger homes. Because Jones is single, she will also target the growing legion of single homebuyers, with whom she can relate and help guide through the home buying process.

COMPETITIVE ANALYSIS

Industry Overview: The Lehigh Valley real estate market is competitive, but not to the point where there isn't any room for a new agent. The industry comprises full-service brokerages to discount brokers, and everything in between. Full-service agents tend to dominate the marketplace, as they have for years, with names like Coldwell Banker and Century 21 dotting the landscape and claiming the bulk of the market share.

Nature of Competition: While full-service firms dominate Jones' marketplace, there has been some erosion not only from discount brokers, but also from those sellers who choose to go it alone (FSBOs), with the help of a real estate agent. Competition for listings is tight, so working with buyers can be a good way to create business since relocations to large companies like Air Products are fairly regular.

Competitors: Key competitors in the market include agents who work for other full-service firms, discount and flat fee brokerages, and "do it yourself" type shops. Competitors also include those home sellers who opt for the For Sale By Owner route.

Opportunities: For new agents that use farming, social, online lead generation sites, and networking, there are significant opportunities both in Allentown, and in the surrounding communities. Situated within driving distance of New York City and Philadelphia, for example, the area has attracted a number of residents who commute to bigger cities daily, but who opt to live in a more rural environment. There are also several large colleges in the region (Muhlenberg and Lehigh University, for example) that attract students who stay in the areas post-graduation.

STRATEGY

Key Competitive Capabilities: Jones is very familiar with the market itself, and knows the characteristics of the various neighborhoods, schools, and other important considerations. She also has a significant network of friends, family, and colleagues who will either work with her when buying or selling a home, or point other customers in her direction. A likeable individual, Jones has the right personality to be a real estate agent.

Key Competitive Weaknesses: Jones never owned her own business, so she doesn't really know what it takes to operate as an independent contractor. She also lacks knowledge of the real estate industry itself, and is unaware of exactly how commission structures, contracts, inspections, and other related issues work.

Strategy: By selecting a brokerage that emphasizes new agent training, Jones will learn about the real estate industry first versus just jumping in feet-first. She'll spend the first few months in the industry either in training, or working with an experienced agent to learn about contracts, inspections, forms, disclosures, and other important issues. Jones will also enroll in her local college's Small Business Development Center (SBDC) introduction to business courses to learn the basics of running a small business.

MARKETING AND SALES

Marketing Strategy: Jones' initial marketing efforts will focus on her own "sphere of influence," or those people to whom she's already connected. She'll add to that stable of potential clients by serving as the "agent of the day" once a month at her office. During that time, she'll receive all incoming calls and emails that <u>aren't</u> already associated with another agent, and be able to turn them into potential clients. Jones will also select a farm area of about 500 homes in her community, and then expand that area as she gains experience in the industry.

Sales Tactics: Using direct mail, email marketing, social networking, her broker's website, door-to-door, and cold calling (as allowed by state and federal do-not-call laws), Jones will target her farm area from various different angles with "Just Listed" and "Just Sold" postcards, as well as general, introductory-type direct mail pieces. Jones will also watch for expired listings and FSBOs in her target areas, approaching them with a clear, crisp sales message based on her own merits plus those of her brokerage, which has been operating in the region for 30+ years.

Advertising: Jones' initial advertising efforts will be limited, but they'll increase as she lists homes for sale. She'll leverage the web by setting up her own website, using pay-per-click (PPC) advertising, and posting Facebook ads. She will also investigate the lead generation sites and determine if this investment would be worthwhile.

Promotions and Publicity: Leveraging local media opportunities, Jones will ask her broker to announce her addition to the team in the local newspaper, in one or more real estate publications, and/or on its blog. She'll watch for opportunities to sponsor events, volunteer her time to local service groups, and create other "newsworthy" happenings that help get her name out into the public eye.

DOLLARS AND CENTS
The Financials: Jones has six months' worth of cash reserves, so she'll need to close her first sale within that time period (or sooner). Working backwards, she'll need to get either a listing or a solid buyer within the next 60 days, then attempt to close the deal within the following 120 days. Jones has a retirement account that she can tap into, if needed,

but her ultimate goal is to be at the closing table to receive a commission check within her first six months in business.

Financial Assistance: To make sure that she's planning both for the immediate future and also for the long-term, Jones will consult with an accountant soon to set up a good recordkeeping system, do tax planning, and figure out some key projections for her new career. When the time is right, Jones will also begin investing in her retirement again, purchase a health insurance plan on her own (or, through a group like the National Association of REALTORS), and take other steps to prepare for her future.

Keeping Records: To track her income and expenses, Jones will use a Microsoft Excel spreadsheet or an online platform like Freshbooks to itemize income sources, as well as business and personal expenses. She's also testing out mobile apps like Mint for personal financial management. On the business side, she'll use a balance sheet, and keep updated cash flow and profit and loss projections in order to see exactly where she stands at any given time. Jones will use this information to make the best and most strategic business decisions.

Sample Business Plan #2: Existing Agent

SUMMARY
Executive Summary: Alex Chavez is a residential real estate agent who has been working in the field for just over two years. He is a full-service agent, who works on a typical commission rate of 6 percent, split with the cooperating broker on each deal. Because he works for a 100-percent brokerage, Chavez doesn't split his side of the commission with his broker, but instead pays a monthly, flat fee to use the broker's physical location and related services. Based in the South Florida city of Coral Gables, Chavez has extensive knowledge of his surrounding community. An entrepreneur by nature, Chavez also has good business

acumen and a handle on the financial responsibilities of running a real estate business, but he's dissatisfied with his results over the last year. Chavez is ready to take his business to the next level.

Business Concept: Chavez is an Accredited Buyer Representative (ABR), who works solely with home buyers. Chavez charges the going commission rate of 6 percent (remember, this rate is always negotiable and never "set" in advance) for his services, and retains all of his commissions on a 100 percent basis (paying a monthly desk fee to his broker of $1,500). He gets the majority of his business through personal contacts, the firm's nationwide referral system, and via online lead generation services. Chavez handles the "buy side" of the deal, helping buyers find the homes of their dreams, negotiating on their behalf, coordinating inspections and disclosures, and providing the buyer with professional advice and guidance in finding the right property at the right price.

Current Situation: Chavez has closed 17 deals during his first two years in the business, for a total of $127,500 in gross commissions. He's now ready to ramp up and do a higher volume of business.

Key Success Factors: Chavez is very familiar with his geographic region, has a large network of potential clients, and knows how to leverage technology to his advantage. Being Hispanic, Chavez is fluent in Spanish and is able to communicate effectively with the Hispanic homebuyers in his region.

Key Challenges: Chavez jumped into real estate and experienced early success, but never took the time to create a solid business and marketing plan. He's been working hard with buyers, but lives deal-to-deal and is unable to predict profit and loss, cash flow, and other important business concepts. The day-to-day tasks keep him busy, but he knows he could be working more efficiently if he were to take the time to create projections and revamp his marketing and advertising efforts.

Financial Situation/Needs: Chavez is married with one child. His spouse earns about $75,000 annually and is able to pay all household bills on that income. She also has health insurance and is investing in a retirement plan. Chavez earned $30,000 during his first year in real estate and $97,000 during the second year.

VISION

Vision Statement: By serving as a trusted resource for individuals and families in his geographic region, and by providing the highest possible service levels to those individuals, Chavez has created a business that supports his lifestyle and allows him to save for the future. By focusing solely on buyers, Chavez channels his energy into a specific aspect of the real estate industry and has become well known for his abilities in this area.

MARKET ANALYSIS

The Overall Market: Through information garnered from the local MLS system and various real estate research firms, Chavez knows that the existing home market is "hot" in South Florida, where homes priced below $450,000 are in big demand, yet very hard to come by. Homes priced in the $450,000 to $600,000 range continue to sell well, with higher-end homes also in demand in the region.

Changes in the Market: South Florida has experienced normal property appreciation rates over the last two years. Right now, he's working in a seller's market, where homes that are priced right are moving quickly (and where more and more of his buyers are getting into "bidding wars" to get their dream homes). The region attracts a great deal of international second-home buyers, as well as relocating professionals, retirees, and those looking for vacation homes in warm climates.

Target Market and Customers: With his office situated in the upscale city of Coral Gables, Chavez helps buyers find homes within the city and in outlying, residential areas. His target customers are often second-home buyers or relocating professionals who use Internet search tools like Realtor.com to search for homes. Chavez also works with some first-time homebuyers from the Hispanic community and international buyers from Latin America, but has yet to fully tap either one of these markets.

COMPETITIVE ANALYSIS

Industry Overview: The South Florida real estate market is extremely competitive, but Chavez has managed to carve out a place for himself by working with a broad range of potential buyers. The landscape comprises full-service brokerages to discount brokers, and everything in between. No one type of real estate firm dominates the marketplace.

Nature of Competition: There's been some market share erosion from the many FSBOs listed on sites like Craigslist plus the discount, web-only, and flat-fee brokers working in South Florida. Competition for listings is tight, which makes buyer representation a popular choice among agents. However, the lack of inventory (particularly in the most desirable price ranges) means buyer's agents like Chavez are forced to deal with multiple offers, strict timeframes, and inspection waiving in order to connect the right buyer with the right home.

Competitors: Key competitors in the market include agents who work for other full-service firms, discount and flat fee brokerages, and "do it yourself" type shops. Competitors also include those home sellers who opt for the For Sale By Owner (FSBO) route.

Opportunities: There are many opportunities for Spanish-speaking real estate agents who truly know the market and can negotiate on their buyer's behalf. There is also a significant opportunity in South Florida within the international buyer marketplace, and among the nation's largest growing group of homebuyers: the U.S. Hispanic population.

STRATEGY

Key Competitive Capabilities: Chavez is very familiar with the market itself, and knows the characteristics of the various neighborhoods, schools and other important considerations. During his first two years in the industry, he received much training and mentoring on the real estate business and is well equipped to run a successful real estate practice.

Key Competitive Weaknesses: Because he never took the time to create a business plan, Chavez is missing out on several key market segments, namely: international buyers and Hispanic homebuyers. Both could benefit greatly from his expertise and honest, ethical business practices. Caught up in the day-to-day aspects of running his business and dealing with a high volume of referrals and leads generated online, this buyer's agent needs to hone his strategy to maximize those key market segments.

Strategy: Chavez will revamp his marketing strategy to target those two groups of potential buyers while also scaling up his own business to accommodate the increase. This can be accomplished by pairing up with another agent whose skills complement his; hiring a full-time, part-time, or virtual assistant; or forming a team.

MARKETING AND SALES

Marketing Strategy: Chavez has largely relied on traditional referrals, word of mouth, and some online leads to bring business to his door. To get the next level, he'll need to expand those marketing efforts to include a few appropriate niches that fit well with his own business style and personal experience.

Sales Tactics: Using targeted advertising online and offline pubs that foreign buyers will likely read; sites that appeal to international and Hispanic homebuyers; and print ads that reach out to such customers, Chavez will attract more potential customers. He'll also continue to work his existing sales channels, thus creating a well-rounded sales strategy.

Advertising: Armed with a small advertising budget, Chavez will create Spanish- and English-language advertising for targeted media outlets (such as local, Spanish-language newspapers in South Florida) that appeals to 1) first-time Hispanic homebuyers who need an experienced, bilingual agent who can educate them and help them navigate the complex process; and 2) international buyers from countries like Latin America, where investors are always interested in the U.S. housing market.

Promotions and Publicity: Chavez will maximize his position as a successful South Florida agent by participating in events and volunteering several hours a month to community causes that reach out to that specific demographic (i.e., Hispanic families that are renting, but who would benefit from purchasing a home but don't know how to go about it). He will also consider teaching a quarterly "homebuyer" course at a local venue. While he can't directly solicit customers through the course, they will remember him and have his literature, information, and website on hand for quick reference when they are ready to buy a home.

DOLLARS AND CENTS

The Financials: Chavez has ample time to build his business while his spouse shoulders much of the household financial burden. This allows Chavez to channel some of his profits back into technology and advertising as he ramps up his business. He will also soon be able to afford either a part-time assistant to handle much of the day-to-day (non-transaction-related) tasks, or contract some of that work to a virtual assistant.

Financial Assistance: Now that his business is in growth mode, Chavez will sit down with an accountant and/or financial planner to decide whether it's time to incorporate his business and set up a retirement account in order to sock away pre-tax dollars for his future. Chavez will also enlist the accountant's help in creating a more formal bookkeeping system, a plan for tax payments, and a quick and easy tracking system for his business' profit and loss.

Keeping Records: To track income and expenses, Chavez will use a Microsoft Excel spreadsheet or a site like Freshbooks to itemize income sources and both business and personal expenditures. Using a balance sheet, he'll keep updated cash flow and profit and loss projections to see exactly where his business stands at any given time. Chavez will use this information when making strategic business decisions.

APPENDIX B

Business Plan Outline

Business plans come in all shapes and sizes, and are generally tailored to the specific company or type of business that you're starting or expanding. Here's a general outline to use when creating your own business plan:

1. **Cover Sheet:** This page should reflect the image of your new company, and include any logos or graphics that you plan to use during the course of business. Use "Business Plan for _____ Company" as the title, and be sure to date the plan.
2. **Table of Contents:** List each section and sub-section throughout the plan.
3. **Executive Summary:** A one- to two-page summary of your business plan. Summarize the key points covered in the plan, and include a complete-but-brief overview of your plan.
4. **Industry/Market Analysis:** An overview of your industry and the market you'll be targeting.
5. **Business Overview:** Description of the products or services you'll be selling, how long your firm has been operating, and a few short-term and long-term business goals.
6. **Ownership and Legal Structure:** A snapshot of the company's ownership structure and choice of business entity (corporation, sole proprietorship, etc.).

7. **Management and Staffing:** Describe the roles that current or future team members and employees will fill in your growing business and detail your plans for adding human resources to your operation as it grows and prospers.

8. **Marketing Plan:** A thorough look at how you will market or "sell" your services to your customers.

9. **Financial Plan:** An honest assessment of how much money you'll need to get this business off the ground and how that money will be used along with a valid reason for using those expenditures.

10. **Business Strengths and Weaknesses:** Your company's strongest points, and how it will grow and thrive in the marketplace.

11. **Growth Projections:** Exactly how you want (and expect) your firm to grow over the next several months, with longer-term projections for the next 2–5 years.

12. **Exit Plan:** A detailed look at how you would plan to sell or otherwise leave the business, when the time comes to do so.

APPENDIX C

More Business Planning Resources

Need more help putting your business plan together? Check out these online resources for more inspiration:

NAR's Guide to Writing a Business Plan
https://www.nar.realtor/writing-a-business-plan

The Balance's Simple Business Plan Template
www.thebalancesmb.com/entrepreneur-simple-business-plan-template-4126711

Bplan's Traditional Business Plan Template
https://www.bplans.com/downloads/business-plan-template/

The SBA's Easy Video Tutorials on Business Planning
https://www.sba.gov/blogs/easy-video-tutorials-business-planning

The SBA's Build Your Business Plan
https://www.sba.gov/tools/business-plan/1

RocketLawyer's Make Your Business Plan
https://www.rocketlawyer.com/form/business-plan.rl#/

ABOUT THE AUTHOR

Having worked as both a REALTOR and a real estate office manager, Bridget McCrea has written five books on the subject (including *Second Homes for Dummies* and *The Real Estate Agents' Field Guide*), and covered both the residential and commercial sides of the industry for magazines like *REALTOR, Bay State REALTOR, Florida REALTOR, Illinois REALTOR,* and *The Residential Specialist*. She enjoys turning complex topics into understandable information that readers can easily apply in their own business ventures. An award-winning journalist, Bridget resides in Florida and is president of Expert Writing Services, Inc.

Made in the USA
Middletown, DE
29 February 2020